NOTES FROM THE INSIDE

WASYL NIMENKO

Brigand
London

Copyright © Wasyl Nimenko 2019
The moral right of the author has been asserted.
All rights reserved. No part of the publication may be reproduced or transmitted in any form or by any means, without permission.
Brigand Press,

All contact: info@brigand.london

Cover design
www.scottpearce.co.uk

British Library Cataloguing-in-Publication Data
A catalogue record for this book is available from the British Library

Printed and Bound in Great Britain by CPI Group (UK) Ltd, Croydon CR0 4YY
ISBN: 978-1-912978-14-4

Wasyl Nimenko was born in Ipswich and studied medicine and psychotherapy in London. He has worked as a GP and a psychotherapist since 1982 when he first started seeing survivors of torture. In 1984 he researched the stress of virtual reality in the first users of the Xerox Star. In 2011 he researched the use of archaeology in the psychological decompression of wounded soldiers and in 2015 he described Post Repatriation Stress Disorder. He has lived in India, New Zealand, Australia and now lives back in England. He has written in depth about Carl Jung, the East and meditation.

Notes From The Inside

Books by Wasyl Nimenko

Invisible Bullets
Searching in Secret India
Searching in Secret New Zealand and Australia
Searching in Secret Ukraine
Searching in Secret Orkney
Searching in Secret Solitude
Stillness
Understanding Stillness

Contents

1.	Living Your Own Way	3
2.	Fear and Catastrophising	7
3.	Ordinary and Simple	13
4.	Being You	17
5.	Relationships	21
6.	Securities	27
7.	Change	29
8.	Resilience	33
9.	Dealing with Difficult People	41
10.	Bullying	51
11.	Torture	57
12.	Abuse	61
13.	Shame	65
14.	Chaos	67
15.	Letting Go	71
16.	Crisis	73
17.	Attitude	77
18.	"Normal"	81
19.	The Importance of Being Weird	85
20.	Being Positive	89
21.	Acceptance	95
22.	Keeping Our Balance	99
23.	Suicide	103
24.	Anger - The 3 R's	107
25.	Kindness	109
26.	Expectations	111
27.	Grief, Adjusting to Death	113
28.	Habits Which Become Addictive	137
29.	Virtual Reality and Technology	147
30.	Living in the Present	153
31.	Creativity	155
32.	What Makes Us Choose	159
33.	From the Mind to the Inner Self	165
34.	Being Still	169

Introduction

We all have difficulties at some time with our health, our wealth, relationships, the point of life or with the inevitability of it. Many of the problems we have with our mind are due to relying on thinking so much that it takes over us so that we can't easily stand back and detach from thinking. Prolonged recurring fear, dark moods and habits which we can't stop, all threaten to overwhelm us because we don't seem to have much control of our mind.

Our most powerful friend to help overcome this is our inner self. These notes are about what you might face whilst on the path turning inside to find your inner self. The notes may be particularly helpful for those of us whose parents were absent or whose parents had problems preventing them spending time with them as their guide as they grew up.

These notes are what I use every day when working with others who find they are in difficult situations. There is no evidence that these notes work other than being happier or seeing a smile or a light in someone's eyes when there hasn't been one for a long time.

The term 'yourself' is used to mean your ego which most people see as us. The term 'your inner self' is used to mean your intangible self, your consciousness, known only by you, which sees and observes your ego.

Notes From The Inside

1. Living Your Own Way

Congratulations, you are in a terrible mess. Congratulations, because the pain and suffering are almost over and you will feel transformed. What a relief and time to be grateful.

Sometimes we have to sit on a mess until we get so fed up with it, we are so uncomfortable with it, we have to move. While we are still childish we can't deal with life well. While we are emotionally too sensitive, we can't relate on all levels. While we lack humility, we can't learn. While we are in denial we can't change. So where do you start?

Your default could be set to be kind to you. Your default could be set to trust you, to help you. Your default may be misplaced and incorrect, but your default is always your choice to adjust. It is from where you change. It is good to occasionally check your default setting. It is good to leave a note to you saying this.

Why don't we leave notes? Why don't they tell us we are perfect with our faults, that we are better than machines can ever be? We can do much of what they do, only more slowly but they cannot be what we are, consciousness. Why are we not told we are perfection and that we need all our mistakes and flaws to learn? Without them we would not have our imagination.

I wish someone had left me notes. Notes about what to avoid. About being quiet and not broadcasting my thoughts so much. About being happy with what we have today. About being happy with what we hear, what we are and with what others say.

Why didn't people leave notes about what is most important in life? Why didn't they say how to be happy instead of commandments saying what we shouldn't do? Why didn't they say the point of life is to live and be happy in your inner self? Not to make others happy or to accumulate material things. Not to be thought of. Not to be thought of as clever. Why didn't people leave notes saying how to be happy inside?

Perhaps people don't leave notes because although there are many clever words to describe us, they are only words, not actually us. They are like a map which is not the actual territory that the map describes. But sometimes words are all we seem to have to communicate. Sometimes our body also tries to tell us what words cannot say but it too cannot say it. We know that something in us sees what our eyes do not see. This something in us which sees is our inner self.

Perhaps we don't leave notes because we have to go our own way, at first from our parents, then straying off paths from others; strong enough to be on our own, with enough fear to keep us alert. Knowledge feeds the brain but doesn't feed the inner self because the inner self cannot be nourished. It nourishes us as we become more conscious of it which makes us happy.

We are not born unhappy, but we dedicate most of our thinking longing for happiness, usually by looking outside for it. We eventually see the happiness we long for is inside us.

So why do we long for something which is already ours, which is inside us? Perhaps it is because our mind is set to default to find happiness in the outside world. We are conditioned and programmed to look for it outside us. But our inner self knows it is inside. Usually we don't look inside until we have had enough suffering and pain in the outside world. We can only find our happiness inside us in our own way. Maybe this is why people don't leave us notes.

When you look for happiness inside, everyone may think you have lost the plot, their masterplan which they think you should be living by. Compared to their standing in the world, you are not a threat. Then the unexpected may appear in their life so that what was meaningless to them becomes the most important thing for them. From enjoying standing above you, their only desire is to try and be happy just sitting with you.

I was determined to find happiness in myself even if it meant looking foolish. I didn't know anything special except perhaps that we are all a little bit messed up and I soon found out that the experts who we think we can rely on to know about happiness do not know.

Early on when I was looking for guidance and training on my own path and a possible career in the world of psychology, a psychoanalyst said I had fear of abandonment. Who hasn't,

I thought. My parents' culture and history were not enquired about, yet their history made me what I am, so I decided psychoanalysis was too intellectual and not helpful. I cancelled my training but he kept on writing to me saying I could do well. I was well, I am well. I cancelled all appointments with him because I had thought, wrongly, there would be some time for the spirit in our sessions, but there was none. It was all about thought; almost perfect logical sequential verbal processing. There was too much concern for the mind and none for the spirit, so I turned on my heels and looked inside for my own way; this way.

When we can take a step back from the picture we seem to be in and see the bigger picture, and then look around to see the rest of the world, we realise we are not alone, how interconnected we are and that we are all fellow travellers. We are all travelling together, all working, skiving and relaxing, trying to make the most of what we have chosen from what is in front of us. We all travel together unaware that we are companions not just for a while but are in this together for good. This is your time, my time, our time. We are in this together.

Notes From The Inside

2. Fear and Catastrophising

Too much of our time we have fear of what will happen. We can even have fear of wasting time when we can never save time, only spend it. This is a conversation I heard in a GP surgery.

'The new water heater is better than that old kettle,' the psychotherapist said to the cleaner. 'Stays hot and saves me so much time. I can pour a cup any time and get more work done. And I don't have to worry about being late.'

The cleaner looked her in the eye. 'I prefer still using the old one, that's why I've kept it. There's nothing wrong with the old kettle. No need to replace it. I can ask someone if they want a brew. Then wait with them while it boils, spending the time having a chat, not trying to save time. You have to wait for a kettle to boil. Waiting for it to boil lets me calm my thinking. Then I'm not a slave to work. Waiting for the kettle to boil, for me is a time to think about other things, not work. I can't make it boil faster because I can't control how fast it boils, so I just relax. The old kettle is great.'

Fear stops us enjoying staying in the present moment. Fear takes higher consciousness down to basic reactions of fight of flight, then even loss of consciousness. Fear blocks and stops smiling and living. It raises a wall to keep it in. It is an isolating draining form of strain. Fear can steer everything for all of our life, or it can be seen and left alone with one single good breath. Fear is a prison made in the mind and is never kind. Fear takes control of your life by taking control of your breath, which controls your body and your brain, which changes your consciousness.

Whatever we do in life, if we can't breathe properly we can't do anything properly.

Fear changes our breathing to shallow faster upper chest breathing. This narrows the arteries in the neck which reduces blood flow to our brain's higher functions. So we are reduced to using our lower basic brain functions such as fight or flight reactions.

When we are frightened, we can only do simple things

because we cannot access our brain's higher thinking functions. A direct way to reduce fear and then get rid of it is to use your breathing to get back control of your body.

By slow deep breathing from the belly, your guts but not the chest, breathing widens the arteries in the neck which increases blood flow to our brain and the brain's higher functions. We can then think more clearly.

It is how you breathe slowly and deeply from your belly that lets you be still and lets your calmness return. Fear is a gut thing that can control your mind, so go with your guts which are in your belly. Your belly is where we breathe best from. Breathing is not only a barometer of fear, but breath control is the best extinguisher of fear.

The lead guitarist in a band came to see me because he was getting dizziness whenever he played certain solo riffs. I couldn't work out why he was getting this until I went to watch him play. When we met later, I imitated his breathing to him and told him it was usually due to fear. He was surprised at first but then he told me that when he was younger, he had a fear of making a mistake playing long riffs. He was able to see that his fear had long gone but his over-breathing had become a habit which stayed. With his increased awareness of this, he prompted himself to breath slowly from his tummy at the start of a riff and his breathing slowed down enough for his symptoms to go.

Fear can also be let go of, like throwing a stone into a pond. You don't hold on to the stone as you throw it, you just let it go its own way. Do you think about where that stone landed after you threw it skimming the water? The less you think about fear the less fear makes you think about it.

Thoughts and feelings come then they go. They are not forever. If we dislike a thought or feeling they can be replaced by others. If it produces fear or loathing, we can let it go then think or feel a different one; maybe think of today as a weekend day, a holiday or a happy moment. Thoughts and feelings are not compulsory.

Thoughts and feelings persist or are freed by our choice and need. You can speak about the fear you saw, the fear you are scared of having again. How it ripped out all the joyful moments of those precious days as a child and how it still stops you having joyful moments. Maybe you are mentally running away and trying to avoid fear. Perhaps you never stop and stay still. Perhaps you don't stop to look inside for your inner stillness as this is what can dissolve your fear. If you keep on trying to find your inner stillness, it will find you.

When the day arrives and you find some inner stillness, you see your inner stillness was here all along and can replace your fear. All you are trying to achieve is the calmness of being still, stopping thinking taking over again. If you move away just a little, turning around, distracted, fear loses its grip and power. But by sticking with fear, it sticks with you.

Fear stops now from being felt because we catastrophise about the future. Fear stops us staying in the present. It stops us experiencing other feelings apart from fear. Fear's enemy is the present. With a still mind we can stay here, and fear is left behind. Letting go of fear of what could happen in the future, releases us from the psychological jail of the future, back into the present.

Otherwise we can catastrophise about anything. Fear is the worst thing to carry around. Unpredictable, fear steals our happiness. Fear of not knowing what to say, fear of failure, fear of not liking ourselves, fear of not being liked, fear of not being approved, fear of abandonment and even fear of fear.

Sequential thinking creates the concept of time by recalling memories of the past and imagining the future. Thinking shows the past and future to be concepts, because our past and future are our thoughts. Our whole life can be spent fighting against thoughts of time, whose inevitable consequences we try to avoid. Wouldn't it be great to be able to still our mind and stop our thinking? Fear is experienced when you don't want it, by thinking of the future. Happiness can't so easily be experienced when you want it but is always inside us. Fear is why we don't do most of the things we could or should do. Trying to be happy is why we do almost everything.

We keep old ways of thinking, believing we can stay

in control. In particular we keep our old fears, thinking we can control our fear. Old ways are chosen as the best because we know them and because they are easy and comfortable. But comfort to avoid change can blind us to what we need to change. We need to own up, give up trying to control and let go. A little less holding on, a little less control, a little less blame and we can let go.

Don't give up trying and keep trying something new. Try looking at what you are not looking for. Let fear of not being happy lead you. Imagine letting your worst fear happen to you in your mind. Imagine you fall over and that everyone sees your underwear. Let it happen several times and you may be smiling at what used to be your biggest fear.

Fear of hesitating, fear of failing, fear of being overwhelmed. Avoiding fear of these ensures fear will get worse. If you don't deal with confrontation, it can deal with you without mercy. If you don't seize the opportunity to confront something, it is turned into a loss. If you give it a go, whatever the result, it can be built on next time, which is progress and a gain.

Fear is behind all our worst behaviours and our dream is a day without it. How can what appears to motivate us seem to be our worst enemy? It keeps us alert and alive being aware of the consequences. Older soldiers don't forget the fear that kept them alive. Sometimes it was right but not now in the middle of the night. Letting go of conditioned fear is strange. Letting go of being afraid is new. Letting go of what might happen takes practice and is conditioning too. Not being afraid in a safe place is normal but can take a lot of practice to feel normal, and then be normal. Normalising lets you feel like everyone else, so you feel the same and not different.

Why is it fear is around all the time and happiness isn't? Perhaps fear is more valuable to our survival, even if it means we are unhappy. Is fear programmed in us from when we are toddlers? Why are we encouraged to be fearful, not our true happy self? If past results show that we only get hurt some of the time, it is better to be happy most of the time than being fearful most of the time. Maybe we could try to get more balance.

We are programmed and conditioned to want to be thought of highly by those above and below us but needing their approval can give control of us to them. Putting and leaving our self-esteem in other's hands is asking and waiting for trouble because disapproval is inevitable. Approval of what we are is only ours. If you have given it away, you need to get it back. Don't expect compliments from others; instead give them to yourself.

Why do so many look down when they are walking? I can understand if its uneven ground, cracked or uneven pavements, and especially if it is because of dog or horse poo. But many of us look down when we are walking out of fear in case when we look up someone will mug us. In America they teach you to tell your burglar or mugger, 'I haven't seen you so I can't identify you.' This lets burglars and criminals win and it explains how the world changes in their favour, and thereby perpetuates fear. Perhaps if we looked them in the eye they might change.

We look down at the ground which eventually will be our longest home, either consumed by fire to become ash or eaten by worms to become soil. We need to look up when we are walking to see our life, where we are going in life. We need to look up to check the ground is safe enough to see we are heading in the right direction. We need to look up to see people eyeball to eyeball. We need to look up to say, 'Hello in there' to the homeless, to strangers, to children, to old people, to say hello to everyone, like and not alike us. Try it for five minutes one day once in your life instead of looking down.

I kept on asking myself, 'How come doubts don't get weaker and why do they seem stronger with the passing of years?' Then I realised it is because my stronger certainty needs stronger doubt to balance it. It is in our nature to have doubts. Their effect is like friends who never stop reassuring us that we are serious about what we have chosen. As night is understood and fades into dawn because the world turns, so doubt melts when we see its positive contribution.

We have endless images inside us which can be pressures to comply with what is outside us. There are pressures to conform, pressures to obey rules and pressures not to fail and not to be a fool. Sometimes it is better to stick with yourself and your own happy foolishness. In the medieval world court jesters were able to play the fool but they were also seen as having wisdom which others could not see so well. It is the same with some comedians today. Perhaps you could risk being the wise fool sometimes?

You could try plugging yourself into an energy supply of positive people. You can burn brighter and shine with other people's energy. They may help you turn fear into fuel and help you live off the dread of panic until even though you search it out, fear cannot be found.

To turn fear into fuel, try and do what makes you scared and you might even get better about what is scaring you. So much so, you can't wait to feel fear and do what you fear because you know performing comes next. Then you might see that the bigger the fear, the better the performance.

3. Ordinary and Simple

Ordinariness is something to aim for because when simple basic things are done and appreciated, they make us happy. When you complicate things, your focus goes and great effort is needed to be ordinary again and unperturbed. When we try to concentrate on one thing only, we can stay focused and calm. Calmness is the best path to aim to be on because over-excitation leads to thinking with fear, anger or a low mood. Keeping our mood simple leads to calmness inside and out.

To have meaning is to have a purpose, although it can be anything. When it involves others, it seems to have more meaning but it is the same, as it is just about us. Some people aim to have enough to live on for the rest of their life and call this being on 'easy street.' There is no such thing as an easy life and easy street doesn't mean life is easy. Easy can mean no work because there is money, but every day still has to have meaning, a purpose with your inner self. We will always search for meaning because it is everything. Sometimes when someone arrives on what they understand as 'easy street' they can have the unpleasant shock that their life has little meaning because being materially successful has been their only aim in life. They may begin a path which others have long been travelling.

Being ordinary, straightforward is what we want, not mystery. We don't want someone else's thousand possibilities about reality; we want to experience reality for our self so that we can be in reality more. Someone else's explanation of why things happened may not help us. When we get things wrong, we don't want resentment, we want acceptance, we want forgiveness. The more straightforward and forgiving we are the more of these we receive.

Although some think that reading is a waste of time it is not because unsuspecting, out of nowhere, like a hidden tiger breaking cover, pouncing on unsuspecting prey, a few lines knock you over and you are changed. Who wrote it is not important. You say to yourself it is what I would like to have realised and said. It makes you see, it makes you think just like a visit to a foreign culture. Remembering, returning home, you compare what you are with what you thought you were before you left; only now the ordinary becomes special.

What is ordinary and what's in the News? The news is more of the same old stuff that is new, just because it is newer. There is nothing new in death because it is old but what is new is a baby. We don't get excited unless news is about one of our own, but news also shows us how much we are alone. News can show us life is more interesting than news because news can be so dull, rolling out repetitive themes. Our own ordinary everyday people and things mean more than the news and touch us much more.

Ordinary things, habits and routines help us more than we know because routines can punctuate pain and suffering with some ordinary normality so at least some normality is felt. Sometimes there is little that can reduce pain and suffering because going through them cannot be avoided in order to move to the next stage. Our simple inner refuge of stillness and silence should always be accessed regularly so it is easier to access at our most difficult time.

Things which I used to describe and report are now not as exciting as the ordinary. The ordinary has been transformed into the authentic, now full of meaning for me. There is no single reason why nature, beauty and what is done simply seem more vibrant than words. We recognise a smile can be worth more than all the words we know. Sophisticated thinking can subtly debase and take us away from what is natural about us. Perhaps also with time, we become more sensitive and drawn to ordinary natural presentations to the senses rather than indulgences of the mind.

Being in ordinary places and doing simple things can inspire us the most. Sometimes when I need fresh inspiration I just go to the bathroom and clean my teeth. What's that got to do with being inspired? Like most places beginning with the letter 'b' such as beach, bed, bath, it is probably the best place to just be to be inspired because it is so simple. There is nothing extraordinary about a bathroom to distract you from being inspired.

    Your whole life so far was all about bringing you here now, right now, so you could see your inner self. Every happening, every journey, every failure and success, everything you hoped for was only ever to bring you here now. That you got here, that you are here now means you can never forget and go back. Once you have seen this moment, you just try and keep it going.

Notes From The Inside

4. Being You

No matter how cringe-worthy or embarrassing you might sound about yourself, it is good to see how you see things, what your attitudes are and what your own rules for living are. You should write some of the strange and weird things down which make you what you are. To help you start finding out about you, here are some of the perhaps odd ways I see certain things.

There are usually two ways I look at our own world. I can see someone as rich for being true to their self and having only just enough money, or poor for only having a lot of money. The Russian or American billionaire on their yacht with their crew of seventeen for security and comfort, who can sail one of their floating mansions into coral bays of sand, and still feel unhappy. Maybe they are unfortunate.

You don't need approval, accreditation licensing or permission to be you. The sun does not ask for forgiveness after it has burnt your skin. It's the sun. The wind does not ask for forgiveness after it has blown away your washing. It's the wind. The rain does not ask for forgiveness after it has wet your face. It's the rain. The snow does not ask for forgiveness after it has stopped you. It's the snow. You should never think of asking permission or forgiveness for being yourself

I don't have reasons for what I'm doing. I don't have reasons why I go to India and I don't have reasons why I've been to India so many times. I don't have reasons why I write, why I'm passionate, why I'm right or wrong. All I know is I'm doing what I'm supposed to do. It's my duty. It's obedience to how I am what I am. There are no reasons to be except to just be. You don't need reasons to just be, so just be.

Finding out who you are can be a shock. It can be a sudden surprise. Of course, what you know about someone you meet is not all there is to them. If you meet them in a family context you may know nothing about their work. If you meet them in a work context you may know nothing about their family. They may have lots of other roles in other settings. It is probably the same for you. We are not only what we first seem on the outside. But on the inside, we are pretty much the same.

When we turn inwards, into the world which is quietly our inner self we see it doesn't try to be something outside itself. We only need to be this, not something else which stops us being fully this.

When we look inside, lots of questions come up about us, and there are some which we can never answer. We can't disown them, but we can try and not see them in a negative way or with any shame. For me I ask why am I sometimes so serious and sometimes sad? Why have I always been so serious? Where does this come from? Was it my orphaned, traumatised Dad? Was it passed on to me from the person I never met, the stillborn brother just before me? Was it my mother's grief about this, her shame about being brought up in a workhouse, or mine about them? After all this time I don't know, and I accept I never will. Is the seriousness really sadness or is it just a seriousness others see in me? I don't know. I accept it as being part of me. It is stuck as part of me. The rest seems fine; just this small crack.

To understand each other and our inner self we sometimes have to try to hear what can't be said, to see what can't be seen, to know what can't be taught; we have to share our self. You are only here once, for a very short time, so it is all up to you. Hello in there, yes you, from me here. What has influenced you to be what you are? My influences have been my family history, our history of poverty, psychological trauma, fighting back then trying to help people worse than me to find happiness within. This is what made me what I am. What about you?

Things about us and the world are not always what they seem. Sometimes the more we make outer progress; the less we make inner progress. The more we have knowledge of the world, the less self-knowledge we have. The less time in the light of the world, the greater the light in the inner cave. Time is a concept so try ditching it for a while as a burden; a distraction from being you, as whenever is always now. Unprompted by material things, the intangible in us calls us to be obedient to complete surrender, true to the own self. This is the most important challenge we face.

If I maintain me, I maintain the world, my world. Whatever maintains the world has its own ways of doing it which I don't understand, and I don't interfere with. I keep my life simple, just getting on with what I have to. My job is maintaining me, and I have my own way of doing it too. My world and I look after ourselves and it is none of my business to interfere with others.

How strange it is to suddenly become aware that our hero is no longer seen as so perfect. It may be that we are also not so perfect or that there is a need to be less like our heroes. There is no-one like an enlightened person. It would be impossible for there to be anyone who is enlightened. An enlightened person would not say it because their enlightenment would make it unnecessary and so impossible. Their enlightenment would abolish the need for ownership of anything including thought. Would you know enlightenment if you saw it? How could you not because it is only you in your reflection.

'I'll tidy my things,' I say when I don't know if I should sing or be silent. 'I'll tidy my things,' I say when I'm not sure what's going on. 'I'll tidy my things,' I say when I want to be alone. When I even think I'll tidy my things, it means I need to be on my own.

When I was growing up everything seemed covered and hidden, so a passion for personal truth and understanding arose. Perhaps what we need the most is a passion for truth in community gatherings to continue being what we are.

Notes From The Inside

5. Relationships

Enough Pain

A couple came to see me because they were arguing about how the husband's two older sisters had been treating him. The sisters were always late when they visited them for a meal. They put the husband down in front of his wife and in front of their four year old daughter and always referred to him as the baby of the family. The sisters were stuck in the past in how they related to their brother and could not see him for what he was now. The couple had repeatedly discussed this with the sisters, but their behaviour remained the same. They had been kind to the sisters but had now had enough pain from the way the sisters tried to humiliate the husband. This caused a lot of frustration and anger which the couple discussed together but the sisters had refused to acknowledge what their behaviour meant to them. What the couple needed was permission from each other to stop the pain by agreeing not to see the sisters again by cutting them out of their family's life.

Desiring happiness is our first desire. Avoidance of pain is next. After seeing what the world is like, after seeing suffering, we look for happiness inside. When you've had enough discomfort, too much pain from being a punch bag, you see you can't do it again. It could be after much change in a family or job. It could even be your relationship with a drug, alcohol or food. Seeing the things you can't change, the time has come for you to move on. With a new threshold of no unnecessary pain we need to ask, 'How can I see them again?' Detachment is often the only way. When we are in a relationship or even a job which is causing us pain, we may need to ask ourselves, 'Have I had enough pain?' If the answer is yes, either we change, they do or we leave the relationship. At the end it usually comes to simply 'change or leave.'

Overwhelming pain of loss of a person you love has no equal except if it happens again with another person you love.

Monstrously out of control feelings wash over fragile circuits of thinking, and then there is standstill. Sometimes all that is needed is a rest from the machinery trying to work out what can only be worked through with more time. With rest is some peace, some time for silence, so stillness inside can be uncovered and recovered.

Our families sometimes appear to make us look smaller just so we can grow taller. When you really needed someone there they made sure they were there, always doing something just giving you time. You never give up on them as you know they exist for you. Except for them you would not exist. The one thing they teach you is to see what you are, where you came from and no matter what, to respect this. Oddly, they showed you to stop anything when you've had enough pain. No point in going back for more, again, again and again. Then you see that they showed you how to pass on what you know and all you have to give: kindness, humility and simplicity.

But some families show us we have had enough pain by causing it. A young mother told me that on two occasions when she had been out with her older sister and some of her sister's friends, that she had felt dizzy and unwell towards the end of the evening. When she challenged one of her sister's friends after the second occasion, the friend told her that her sister had spiked her drink with vodka. She met her older sister who didn't apologise and said it was just a joke. But the younger sister realised it was not just a joke; it was an attempt to humiliate her so her older sister could look more important. She phoned her sister but her sister did not answer her calls so she wrote a letter telling her sister their relationship was over.

Eventually we say, 'I've got to stop this now as I've been hurt so many times. I've had enough pain and I don't want more from them ever again. I've given them too many chances and every time I got mugged. At first I didn't acknowledge the emotional pain but now my feelings can't be mugged again. This is being clear about me doing things so I don't get hurt. I am giving up being polite with them. It is about me not getting mugged again.'

When is now? When will you say you have had enough pain, that you don't just want to be the giver again? When will you say they are not going to take off you again? When will you think of you first and say no? When will you say no they can't come and stay? When will you say I've had enough, today is the day?

When will you wake up how you went to sleep and say yesterday was the first day of me saying no? No becomes the most positive word. It changes the uncomfortable feeling inside into positive feelings of protecting yourself. You start looking for times to say no just to feel better about saying yes to you. Then you see why so many people do it all the time and say no. It makes them feel good.

Sometimes our thinking doesn't work fast enough to save us because we have too much trust in our own expectations of us and others. So we have to change our expectations. Some people do not care about us. They never will. We have to let our expectations go.

Some expectations are simply habits and we have to let go of them. I try to look outside and inside to see how much I expect. The weather today is good outside. Inside I'm full of change. This is what I need. What I am is not anyone else's to have to cope with but sometimes my coping has to close its eyes and let the weather just be wild inside. Today is like that. I will bury myself in the silent intense activity of stillness and wait to accept my expectations have to change.

When you step across a railway line, it's not the buffet car that kills you, it's the engine. When you relapse into an old habit, it's not the second bottle of booze or repeatedly taking a drug that does the damage, it's the first one that gets you. When you see that small sign, perhaps a light of hope, it's not what comes after it that gets you; it's that small light of hope which can guide you forever back home. Every addict's family and friends know this.

Friendships

Mental scars are not something we point our finger at unless they are ours. Damage is a cost some of us pay for experience which allows us to grow. The battle-hardened, the scarred and the damaged are stronger than the sheltered. Only the damaged recognise the path which the overprotected only occasionally notice. Someone who has mental scars, who understands the language of suffering, is a better companion than the shielded. Finding the path and staying on it needs the right companions who are similarly battle-hardened and equals.

Stick with happy people not with partying people. Stick with people who are interesting to know because they are also interested in knowing you, who you feel good about being with.

When you meet someone they are not just a face with a smile and a body. There is an unmeasurable amount of influence going back decades. There are important ancient family histories, stories, legends and facts, scandals and gossip mixed with truth and beauty. The result is what you see.

We are not just workers, our concerns not seen, our personal caring touch not valued because it has no price. Perhaps our personal hidden touch kept secret from the powers that seem to rule, lets us rule our own heart better. How can you so easily be trapped working unless you are stuck down a mine? You may be stuck in a job but it's your choice to stay in that job. How can you be trapped with someone unless you are conjoined or handcuffed? If you can walk away, it is you who choose to stay or leave.

When someone doesn't listen; stop talking. If they ever want to listen they will find you. Repeating yourself, raising your voice to attract their ears won't help if they can't hear or won't listen. It may be time to accept them as they are and move on.

Thirty years ago I was frustrated that I was aware of my ignorance of relationship dynamics. Now knowing them better I am frustrated because you cannot learn them any quicker. I learnt that my sense of intimacy had changed, was changed, but I didn't know it. I didn't know intimacy because what I thought I knew was only my own projection of what I had always wanted. I didn't know this. It wasn't what I thought it was. Thrown into chaos, not knowing if there was anything to salvage, the tears flowed and flowed because now I knew that I didn't know intimacy. Gathering myself, I let go and didn't cling on. Detachment with love is the only way, going our ways, together, forever.

There is nothing as difficult as relationships as they cannot be predicted and they cannot be controlled. They cannot be what you want them to be because there is always the other who has their say. They can change or not, give you the greatest sadness and joy but they are not yours but shared.

Perhaps there are no relationships, they may just be projections, our best guess of what we think is there, often what we want to be there. Relationships can be projections of thinking someone cares when we don't even know what we care for.

Relationships can be two people sending out projections which they believe. How could we be someone else's invisible projection? How do you see who is really there especially if you can't see your inner self?

We think our children are leaving us but feelings, attachment and memories reinforce this is not true. Our children do not leave us. They are going their own way finding all the things we have reflected on as we leave them.

Notes From The Inside

6. Securities

Maybe security is learnt through insecurity, stability learnt through instability, surrender learnt through fighting, detachment through attachment and happiness learnt from suffering.

When I reflect on the opportunities I have turned down which would have made me materially secure, the decisions left me materially insecure but richer inside and I have been happier as a result. When I reflect on betrayals which left me bruised, although they seemed like losses, they let me learn more about trust. It seems no matter what, I remain outwardly insecure. Maybe it gives me a hunger, a passion, perhaps because I have chosen to carry on surrendering. Perhaps outer happiness and security are sometimes not the best friends and for some of us they are impossible friends.

Perhaps how you arrive at the graveyard is not important. It is what you arrive as. Did you have a good journey and arrive in your own happy way? Did you have happiness or did you have pain? Did you pass anything on and has everything you had gone? Are you happy to be here, relieved all is done or did your life leave other people's lives undone? The worst thing is to arrive as the richest person in the graveyard.

It is so easy to default to feeling overshadowed, even a failure in comparison to someone who has been successful in the world. But that is only until we turn inwards and see the treasures we have inside which they have declined.

On the whole, life is mostly predictable because we follow or reject what we are given. We take risks or are conservative but most people follow what their parents taught them. The joys we experience are the same for almost everyone. Our suffering, our diseases and death are not predictable but are inevitable. We divide up into various groups for mutual support as our parents did. Perhaps the most important thing is to be happy and have as much joy as is possible with our self and others because material things do not makes us happy.

Being attached to everything, you cannot be true to your inner self. Having everything you want money can buy is being poor because all you have is money. To let go of everything is to be at home everywhere because you are homeless. To let go of everything you are the richest person because you have no attachments. Perhaps a happy person could be best defined as 'a person with no wants.'

Seeing your thinking is wrong and you are not as connected like society makes you think you are is a shock. But this can let you relate to everyone easier as you realise you are something deeper than your thoughts, when you see you are not just your thoughts. The most elite of company, fascinating conversations, adventures and descriptions revealing interesting ideas can be too painful to endure. All invitations to encounters like this have been avoided so successfully that I can say with happiness that I am now not invited. My security is secure.

When the last act of helping has been monetised, man has to change and turn around or he is not man. Every move can be mechanised and monetised. Every breath you take can be sanitised and monetised. Preventing monetising of everything could begin to enrich the homogenous cultureless future with at least kindness. Perhaps the turning point of man could begin with being kind and helpful, with gratefulness being the most sought after reward.

We have created a world of seduction, passing pleasures and dreams of security, which is a clever illusion. Our apparent world seems to be always changing like our thoughts, which ceaselessly come and go unless stopped. Only when they are stopped is our inner world seen.

The material world not only doesn't seem to be my best friend, it is not. The people who aspire to this are also not, so who is my friend? Well there are less than a handful who care for my inner world. I considered being more connected with the outer things of the world but when I saw what it was like, I packed my inner bags and I spend as much time as possible on the path of inner security. It has not let me down.

7. Change

Imagine there's no imagination, only what is now. If we couldn't think of alternatives how would anything have changed? Change happens because of imagining that things can be better than how they are. How often do you imagine changing how you are so you can be different to how you are now? Perhaps what can be changed the most is seeing what you actually are.

Desiring happiness is our first desire. Avoidance of pain is next and seems to be our best motivator encouraging us to do things we would not necessarily consider. Alternatives are not often thought of before the threat of pain and are usually only considered when there is too much pain and we see we don't want to endure any more pain.

The best place to go and change is not on holiday because you take your head with you. It is not on the holy mountain or in a monastery. There is only one place to go to change; inside.

To begin the process of change I have to question myself. Perhaps there are influences which I still need freedom from or an individual who has too much power. After all, even the English game of cricket can take a new form, so what about me? Perhaps take a look at your attitudes. Are you pretty rubbish at resentment, at being aggrieved and bitter because it keeps on coming back with things you just see as black? The things you want to change about others may actually be attitudes in you to them. If you look at these you can see and decide what you can't change and what you can change, which is your attitude. If you can do this, you have already changed.

At first we don't like change and we avoid change simply because we fear what will happen to us if we change. We are not taught how to prepare for change. Before we change gear in a car we have to adjust our setting by getting into neutral; only then can we move on in a new gear. We are not taught how to be thoughtless and still because we are not taught how to just be with our own inner self. We need time of being in neutral too; a time of adjustment which we need to recognise and accept.

How many times do we come close to death in our lives

to see what we are? How many times do we have to learn how to relate so that we default to feel love in our hearts not hate? How many times do we travel different paths until we finally see only by giving up all paths we are free?

Giving up expectations cannot be stopped because we always expect something, especially life, but most expectations are wishful thinking. Trying to change someone is always more difficult than self-change and can be impossible, so it is easier to start with yourself. Changing our self is the only place to start change.

Sometimes we can contribute more by using our influence on ourselves rather than on others. We can give more if we give more to ourselves rather than to others. We can help more if we spend more time on our own rather than with others. We can change things more if we change ourselves rather than others.

Maybe we could stop trying to persuade someone before persuading our self. Maybe we can stop trying to correct someone before correcting our self. It is easy to look out at others and criticise them. But how difficult it is to look inwards and see what is good and bad, positive and negative about what we are before we criticise anything or anyone.

Some things only work one way; like only being able to help someone after you have helped yourself. If the plane you are flying in has a sudden loss of oxygen pressure, you have to put your mask on before you can help others. Most importantly you are only able to love someone after you love yourself.

When you try to understand someone, whatever they say, whatever they do, don't only react with your mind, respond from your heart. They may never change so step off the merry-go-round. Let it all stop. To understand someone, pretend to be them for an hour to feel their weight or lightness. Are there things holding them down or maybe things that should be? Do these make them repeat what they do to others and to you? Is it up to others and them to change or is it just up to you?

Sometimes everything in our life seems to be changing and we can't find any ground to stand on and feel secure and safe. Thinking, feelings and behaviour don't change without a cause. Happiness and mental health don't change much without a cause.

When change is happening and we don't seem to have any control over it, we need to look inside and see there is nowhere to turn to except to what we know, what is inside us. We hope it will end well as sometimes we actually do know we have no control. We can be near to being on our knees begging and praying for it to end well. Perhaps this is the only way we are able to surrender, to give up every single thing and just be our inner self. It may be the best place to start.

Maybe we can't become anything only be what we already are. Perhaps we do not change; we only see what we are, so we can become conscious of what we already are.

Put another way, no matter how much we try to change, we cannot become what we are not. We can only be what we are. It is all as it is meant to be. I can't become because I already am all I can be, which is my inner self. But what I can change is being conscious of it. This is real change and is removal of ignorance.

One thing we know is that we have been asking the same question about ourselves for several thousand years and we are still asking it. Is it time to rely less on thoughts and just be happy? Sometimes we see that there is no cure for life. How could there be? What would it be? More life, a different life? Changed consciousness?

Change can completely transform what we think can't be changed. We easily forget that out of man's darkness comes his own light. The unmaterialistic reformed thief is often the most honest. The recovering reformed addict is often the most sober minded. The reformed adulterer is often the purest. The repentant reformed murderer is often the gentlest.

When you are in darkness you can't see any light because your vision is unreliable and you try not to stumble and fall. When light arrives, you adjust and forget the fear of stumbling and falling, then darkness arrives again and you try not to stumble and fall. We really do not know when either will go or come, which makes us good at adapting to change.

Most creatures like us seem to be ones of hope. In times of crisis they hope and look for ways out. In calmer times they try and maintain the calmness, living in hope that things will stay good and not change. We all try to maintain our happiness.

When we are not watching or listening things are usually ready to change. We think they have changed but when we look at them again from another point of view, we may see that it is us who have adjusted and changed.

Perhaps we can stop trying to live only by thinking and instead live by authenticity. Being able to see the faults of the world but not our own may be easier but it is not being responsible because change has to begin inside.

8. Resilience

The Korean War

At the end of the Korean War a study by the US Army Medical Corps found that of the 7,190 captured American soldiers, 38% died and under torture over 30% collaborated with the enemy. The study concluded that the high number of American deaths in captivity and the high collaboration rate with the enemy were due to the collapse of morale resulting in the loss of allegiance to their country or to one another.

The US Army Medical Corps also found that of the third largest represented nation in the Korean War, the Turkish Army, not a single Turk died in captivity and not a single Turk collaborated with the enemy under torture. They concluded that the Turks' resilience was due to discipline, pride in their group and an unbroken chain of command. Clearly the Turks had a glue which held them together as individuals and as a group. It was more than just discipline and pride; they had powerful shared beliefs like their religion and their traditions such as wrestling.

After the Korean War it was obvious that the Turkish prisoners were resilient and the American prisoners were not. Astonishingly, instead of finding out what made the Turkish prisoners resilient and looking at this in American soldiers, the Americans came up with the "Code of the US Fighting Force," which consists of statements about resisting and evading questioning during torture. Essentially it says that 'I am an American and I will never surrender and if captured I will only give my name rank, serial number and date of birth.

It states expectations of behaviour but does not indicate how these are achieved. Over the years it sowed the seeds to form the modern specialist training known as SERE.

SERE is an acronym for Survival Escape Resistance Evasion which is a course you have to endure to be military air crew, Special Forces, MI5 or MI6. As well as America, SERE is taught in the UK, Canada, Australia, and New Zealand.

Inconvenient a truth though it may be, SERE is also a standardised way of teaching people interrogation methods (how to torture others) which are prohibited under international law.

You volunteer (without giving consent) to be tortured by your colleagues who are trained experts, so you can learn how to endure it and how to do it too.

It begins with being let loose on Bodmin Moor and having to avoid being captured. When they capture you, they blindfold you and put you in the back of a truck and drive you back to the military base. You are stripped naked, and then experience genital humiliation by a blond female alongside being hosed with water. You are given no food and no sleep for days. You are made to stand at first with bright lights in your face and then made to stand hooded in darkness. You are slapped a bit but not badly beaten. Once an individual actually did escape from this. He was labelled defective and a failure. They said there was something wrong with him and he was discharged and forced to return to civilian life.

It is easy to show on a course what might be done to you if you are tortured but creating the glue that makes individuals resilient and stick together cannot be simply taught. It has to be the centre of what they are.

The basis of resilience is meaning. After the Second World War, Viktor Frankl, an Austrian survivor of Auschwitz said in his book, 'Man's Search for Meaning,' that the survivors or the concentration camps were the ones who had a sense of meaning, whilst those with no sense of meaning perished.

The All Blacks

When we are part of a group we can endure things with more strength because we get more commitment from being part of something which is bigger than us.

A good modern example of the anatomy of resilience

is the New Zealand All Blacks Rugby team which is the most successful rugby team in history, winning 86% of their professional matches. The team share three identifying values which give them resilience; the New Zealand Nation, the specific All Blacks culture and principles of the Maori culture.

This unique triple strength glue which holds them together as a team is expressed as the Haka, which is a ceremonial choreographed dance performed right in front of the opposing team's faces just before a match begins. It is an ancient traditional Maori dance of male warriors. The Haka has different forms for different uses and the All Blacks use the Haka that is traditionally used just before battle begins.

The Haka is a ferocious display of their aggressive, utterly defiant team spirit designed to intimidate the opposing team. It includes the whole All Blacks team slapping their hands against their thighs, stomping their feet, protruding their tongues and showing the whites of their eyes, whilst making various cries and grunts.

Any team standing watching and listening to the Haka are intimidated not just because it is usually associated with the traditional battle preparations of male warriors but also because they realise they are not just playing the New Zealand rugby team. There is a sense they are confronting the power of the All Blacks and also the Maori culture. They sense that the New Zealand rugby team is held together by more than just being the national rugby team and that they are held together stronger than they are. Other teams find it difficult to learn how to acquire this glue because it is what the All Blacks are.

The All Blacks clearly demonstrate through the Haka that the glue which holds individuals and groups together is meaning, which others observe as resilience.

Psychological Decompression

To maintain a group's morale after a ferocious battle there needs to be a time of psychological recovery, reflection and renewal of the things that hold individuals or the group of people together. In the military this is known as psychological decompression.

In the British Armed Forces, immediately after a tour of duty, the sense of working together as a team is usually reinforced by a period of psychological decompression for several days. It is a winding down time at a 'staging post' in Cyprus on the way home tour which involves various forms of entertainment, time on a beach, barbecues and the controlled availability of alcohol.

Although psychological decompression is routine at the end of a tour, there is no evidence which shows it to be either beneficial or detrimental; basically because no one has ever looked at it and researched it. Psychological decompression is now generally accepted but only takes place because most soldiers see it as a positive post-tour event.

In 2011 when I was working with injured members of the armed forces who had just returned from the frontline of a war zone with various psychological and physical injuries, I noticed that most of them had become isolated and were showing symptoms of fear, isolation and loneliness as well as symptoms of traumatic stress.

I suspected that they were doing so badly because they had quickly become isolated from the team they worked with and were now lacking the support from the camaraderie and team spirit which had just recently held them together. All of these people had returned straight from the front line back to their military camp and had missed the traditional psychological decompression in Cyprus. Their resilience was very low, which in the Armed Forces is often looked at only in terms of morale.

I suspected that the soldier's intuition about the positive benefits of psychological decompression was correct and so I decided to do an experiment. I looked at 28 of these soldiers on an archaeological dig on their old training ground over several days, under conditions which mimicked conditions of the psychological decompression they had all missed. I wanted to see if their psychological states improved after working together again as a team. They rated themselves the day before leaving for the dig and the day after returning on five standard psychological rating scales.

The dig was a 4–5 hectare 2700-year-old 3 meters deep feast midden (rubbish tip) which was formed over approximately 100 years at the end of the Bronze Age.

The whole group camped outside with the soldiers who were overseen and informally supervised by 7 professional archaeologists as they worked in groups digging and sorting material; most of the material consisted of fragments of pots and animal bones as well as flint fragments and evidence of making iron. The pottery was particularly interesting to the soldiers not just because of its age and that they were the first to touch it in 2,700 years but some of it was patterned and also some pieces had the fingerprints of the potters on them which were visible as well as palpable. Each of the two digs took 5 days and turned out to be 'find rich' in that 10,500 pieces of pottery and bones were found, washed, recorded and removed over two five day digs.

There was a feast-like supper every night, initially with a 'two can' limit (a limit of two cans of beer per soldier per night). This limit was removed on the third night when there was a barbecue and a quiz in a nearby barn, the rationale being to mimic feast-like conditions and other aspects of the psychological decompression in Cyprus, with the exception of the beach.

This small pilot research concluded that this exercise of psychological decompression significantly helped isolated and distressed battle injured soldiers return to effective operational roles within their regiment. Essentially it helped to restore their resilience and morale.

The results showed a mean of 13%–38% improvement across the five psychological reporting scales. The 7 civilian archaeologists reported improvements in the soldiers' self-esteem, morale, team-working and sense of general well-being.

The results of the pilot research (jramc.bmj.com/content/160/4/295) were presented to the head of the British Army as support for 'Operation Nightingale' to get the go ahead to be rolled out across the Armed Forces. As a result of this, shortly after the exercise was completed, the archaeologists formed the Defence Archaeology Group to use the technical and social aspects of field archaeology in the recovery and skill development of soldiers injured in conflict around the world. The Armed Forces acknowledged the significance of psychological decompression.

One of the most important things the traditional period of psychological decompression probably does is to reinforce the glue which holds soldiers together. Because it takes place in Cyprus in an informal social setting, it helps to ensure that everyone accepts and agrees about what has happened to them as individuals and as a group.

This probably helps them to think and act more confidently that what held them together before and during their tour of duty is still there. Psychological decompression may well help restore and maintain their sense of meaning and their world view which are all part of resilience.

Resilience through Solitude

Your sense of 'yourself' can mean your ego which most people see as you. But 'your inner self' can mean your intangible self, your consciousness, known only by you, which sees and observes your ego.

Resilience always comes back to meaning and is what we mean to ourselves. Our commitment to our own meaning is the most important influence on our resilience. Resilience is about being your inner self, so you are not changed by anything and involves being able to return to your inner self no matter what.

You may have difficulty with your health, your wealth, relationships, the point of life or with the inevitability of it. You might rely on thinking so much that it takes over you, so you can't easily stand back and detach from thinking. It can seem you don't have much control of your mind because of prolonged recurring fear, dark moods and habits which you can't stop which can all threaten to overwhelm you.

Your ego may be damaged by your upbringing, by circumstances, by prolonged fear, dark thoughts or habits or by others and your thinking may appear strange and unusual for you. No matter what happens to you, your most powerful friend to help overcome this is your inner self.

It may look like your thinking is broken by wounds and you have fragmented and broken down and are unable to function. But this may not be the case. Just like a physical wound to the skin which has formed a scab over it to protect the healing process underneath it, psychological wounds can be hiding inner change and healing which are encouraging new growth.

Sometimes it is only when you view underneath what has been damaged and what is newly forming that you see it has been developing your potential. It can be a resilient person, who has all along just been waiting to express their inner self.

There is a solitude which brings happiness unaffected by the intentions and actions of others; it is withdrawal into and enjoying our inner self. This safe shelter is a refuge and used to be known as asylum. We have always known we need to be able to get back to our own inner harbour. Sometimes we need others to point us in the right direction to stop what we are doing, so we can have a break from the outside world and our own thinking.

There was an interesting study reported in the British Medical Journal in July 2002, (www.ncbi.nlm.nih.gov/pmc/articles/PMC1123553/) which showed that a six week stay at a Hindu temple in Tamil Nadu, India, produced the same improvement in severe psychiatric disorders as a month long course of standard psychiatric drugs such as Chlorpromazine or Risperidone. Of the 31 people who took part and were evaluated by psychiatrists, 6 had delusional disorders, 23 had paranoid schizophrenia and two had bipolar disorder.

The patients only attended a simple morning prayer for 15 minutes and spent the days helping with routine temple work. They showed an average 20% improvement on a standard psychiatric tool the 'Brief Psychiatric Rating Scale.' This was a dramatic improvement which would be expected after four weeks of taking standard psychiatric drugs, and it had come from being in a supportive non-threatening environment. These results which have been largely ignored lead to serious questions about the powerful resources we have inside our self and with others which we could use instead of the continued use of psychiatric treatments.

    I would endure a whole week of strain for one happy day and if that is what it takes to do it, I would do it again and again. Happy days are rare as there is so much to do. Knowing happiness is hidden but always there is the main key to resilience.

9. Dealing with Difficult People

Avoid the Negative

I have never been able to find any useful guidance for dealing with difficult people, because there doesn't seem to be any. There are only general points which may help us in some situations but not in other situations. Dealing with difficult people is nearly always about dealing with our self. So when we are in a difficult situation dealing with difficult people, we have to remember that we are the most difficult people we have to deal with.

I was eight years old and on a long leisurely walk in the country with my elderly grandfather when we came across a large pile of fresh cow dung. He stopped, looked down and pointed at it, 'You can learn a lot about some people from that pile of dung.

'Like what? I asked,

'If you don't step in dung it won't stink.'

I took this as not getting involved with the negative. But now it means not getting involved with things that don't concern me. It means not complicating my life when I don't have to. It can remind us to keep certain people out of our lives and not let them in. It means having a people boundary which you control.

I tend to stay away from certain people as they can cause unimaginable trouble which you could not make up. If you have not had enough trouble, mix in until you are in too much trouble, perhaps only then you will be very careful of your inner self.

A crook needs to be crooked to succeed. They are like this because they don't know how to be happy being straight. They can create gossip and smokescreens to hide what they are really like. They can present as honestly doing good when it is all part of their acting. If you don't play their game, if you don't play with them and you are not playful, they have to find another playmate because they are compelled by what they are. Remember if you don't step in a cowpat, it won't stink.

People who use and abuse others approach them with

friendliness, promises and kindness, not hostility. Once fooled, because we are sensitive, we should train to be more defensive, cautious and guarded in how we respond as we can still be fooled and attacked. We need strong unmovable defences. Not trusting is the most important thing to learn about everyone else. Not trusting is the most difficult thing because it is learnt only through pain received from trusting someone. Not trusting is vital for survival, vital for enthusiasm because you have to trust only you. Perhaps it is better to engage with people who perhaps don't trust others.

Don't Forget the Positive

Learning how not to get involved in things which don't seem to concern us is a choice and sometimes we feel compelled to get involved out of passion. One of the worst regrets we can ever have is having done nothing when we could have done something. Things may be more of our business than we can see at first because sometimes we have to follow our heart. Sometimes getting passionately involved with something which at first didn't seem to be our business can be the most positive thing we will ever do for us and others. It can change our whole life. Through it we can find our own meaning.

Keep Focused and Concentrate on You

Most of the time I feel passionate that we are refugees in a world which is still trying to get rid of us, a world which does not support the contemplative life, a world where there have to be results. The intangible is becoming the rarest of all and the intangible needs protecting as much as our planet does, so that we can continue to pass it on.

The biggest difficulty we face is always keeping the main aim the main aim. A sustained attack of thoughts lasting one month can be so distracting and consuming that it can take you to your limits of coping. It can be any distraction by another person, someone challenging you, bullying you or stealing from you who you can't formally stop, someone who plays a game. Their game interferes with you by interfering in your control of your thoughts. Keeping a steady aim as things continue, your victory is more certain than you can see. Keeping the outer aim steady, try and retreat inside to keep the inner aim as the main aim. Try and find some silence so you can more easily have some inner stillness. Slowing the breath will eventually slow the thoughts, keeping the main aim the main aim.

The reason to be able to be still is that there is no rescue from life as being alive is dangerous and only we can protect our self. No one else can rescue us from life because we are meant to be here. We have been placed here by people to live this dangerous life. Protecting our self from depending on others protection and doing it our self brings some peace to this dangerous beautiful life.

Step Back and Detach

When you are troubled, stand back from the waves trying to overwhelm you like a tsunami rising up at you and take steps backwards up the shore getting to higher ground. Keep on stepping backwards getting higher from the waves. Finding yourself on higher ground, let go of everything lower down. Look around you, seeing everything that makes you happy. Enjoy the happiness on higher ground, the silence, the stillness. This is where you belong.

When we overthink, detachment is separating ourselves from others. Detachment is separating our processes from other people's processes. Detachment is separating our thoughts from other people's thoughts. Detachment is separating our feelings from other people's feelings. Detachment protects us.

Intolerable situations can be other people imposing aspects of their lives on ours so that our life is unhappy or we are not fulfilling our self. Either we change and move or they do. Yes it is correct; sometimes I've not been able to stay in some jobs as long as I had expected. When I found out what was happening I found it difficult to not protect the defenceless person I was in that job. Usually I didn't have the reins of power; I only had the path to the door which looked like irresponsible foolishness.

Being true to our self is often exchanged for comforts, material security, a large pension with a comfortable retirement and awards. It has not been a problem for me to speak and walk away. Even now, though I feel psychologically out in the cold, I am warm inside and always sleep well at night.

You cannot negotiate to make meaningful progress with certain types of people because even inevitable, painful consequences may not move them. If they keep on coming back, they usually need to be psychologically firmly disposed of and often repeatedly.

Take Time to Take Stock of Everything

There are some periods of slow deep inner change which may not yet be worked out in thoughts so there is unrest, unhappiness, worry and we are often alone until it is processed. Processing change can't be rushed even if it is instant change because accommodation to the change has to be met on every level and has its own time.

On our own, our thoughts transform into words what we want to say. Only then how we will live our days can be worked out.

Recovery of your own life may never occur but a crisis is usually the best thing to ever happen. It lets you see what you lost, what you can't get back or what you don't want back. It lets you ditch the unnecessary. Reclaiming what you see as yours can then be followed by restoration of feelings, of clear thinking, of balance, of health, of friendship, of strength, of hope, of your spirit. Some days have almost everything you could have thought of to be perfect, and then you are surprised because someone makes you happier.

Usually in the thick of it we can't see what it was we started by what appeared like a small decision to stand our ground. Complexity does not diminish our integrity but it can act as a smoke screen to hide things from us and distract us. Other people's secrecy and deception, when unmasked, only highlight our integrity. Usually unless you know something they don't, don't say it unless they ask and even if you do know something they don't, and don't say it until they ask again. Leave those alone who don't ask for help as they will be looked after by their self or someone.

Our inner self care is vital. Reprogramming ourselves every night, like washing our faces of all the dirt we have accidentally picked up, is essential to keep us our authentic self. Reprogramming ourselves has to be done every day if we let ourselves be programmed by information from people, the media or the selling of everything by everyone.

The joy and problems we have with others are a function of living with others and do not go. The joy and problems we have with our self with being in the world do not go. Both joy and problems with others and our self and just being happy with our self, are being vibrantly alive.

We should not forget that we are complicated but always want to be explained simply. We are happy to babysit a lion cub. Happy to process information on computers. Happy to work for peace. Happy to help. Happy to love and happy to die. We are at times incomprehensible. So, with everyone and everything, ask what is good. Seek out the positive not anything negative. Life is a range of many different experiences. A smile, a child, a stranger waving to you on the road, daydreaming, making a new friend. Skip one step a day like a child.

Everything comes with its own appointment. Answers come in their time, not ours. We can't change allotted appointments because we want timely satisfactory answers. Just being occupied whilst waiting for the answer ensures we are ready for whatever it gives us. Courage is not on tap but comes from a challenge and we are not ready until it passes our way.

Your opponent is always your best teacher, your best friend and often a hidden part of you. Treat your opponent with more respect above everyone else as they can teach you more if you find out why they oppose you. They may lay down their life to show you this. Even though you may not see this, you cannot exist fully without them. The most cunning, sadistic, greedy, selfish, dishonest, wealthy person with no principles taught me more than anyone about what I want and don't want.

If our opponents are our best teachers so what did mine teach me? They showed me I am still passionate about what I do. Through betrayal, dishonesty and gossip, an opponent can ignore responsibilities and abuse power so it becomes a force against you, weakening you or correcting and strengthening your weaknesses. It is good to be passionate about integrity, about being kind, about not being late, about respect. It is good to be passionate about not lying, about being direct, open and honest, about simplicity, about hard work.

My passionate reactive nature is from my parents and some people find it too much but it doesn't worry me because it is only me trying to speak. I have seen injustice and I have had injustice. It is incorrect to not act to not speak, and if ignored, to not act and speak repeatedly. I am frequently left a little disappointed others don't trust my over-passionate nature.

When you leave your family it can be the right thing. You can continue to lovingly grow together seeing and being with each other. But some families are dangerous company and you have to escape. Some are so distressed and incapable they dump you somewhere. Some families stop you getting on and won't let you leave, so when they keep on pulling you back, it may be time to separate. We have to find our own life letting them continue theirs. Giving them their stuff and dealing with ours gives us freedom to let all our lives blossom.

Warning Signs

Telling someone they are stressed out, or they are unhappy or angry are none of your business if you are not going to help because if you tell someone without offering help, you are making them think about you, not them. This can be taking not giving. It can be passive aggression.

Making someone feel stupid is a wounding that must not go unchallenged. Telling others doubles the wound and doubles the violence. Making someone feel stupid is a wounding that must not go without them understanding their error in the use of authority. Making someone feel stupid is a wounding that must not be repeated as no opportunity for a second chance should exist. Making someone feel stupid is a terminal event.

Being ignored means not being regarded with enough importance. Being ignored means not being taken seriously enough. Being ignored means manners have been dropped as a statement. Sometimes it is best to ignore being ignored because sometimes it is the end.

Someone behaving badly affects us, and then they make us feel awkward for telling them, so we feel guilty. They don't change but they try to turn our guilt into a problem so that we are the bad person. As it is not usually our issue we can leave them to the consequences.

When relating to someone is strained with lack of agreeableness and conscientiousness, try and remember to think of the triple personality the Dark Triad. For a Dark Triad's success their Machiavellian deception doesn't use force but uses charm to interpersonally manipulate everyone as they are unprincipled masters of deception. Their Narcissism makes them seem superior even grandiose but they overdress to look good. Their psychopathic coldness but impulsive love of danger sees them take risks in leading. The one in a hundred people with the Dark Triad personality will exploit and take every opportunity to get what they want no matter what. Watch out for them as they can seem like the most charming people.

Step Back and See the Bigger Picture

Whatever I have done or not but others say I have, is their thinking. It is known by me but thought by others. Whatever I have been or not but others say I have is their thinking. It is known by me but thought by others. Others' investment in judging me may enrich their world of securities or may make it look like they overpower me or make their ego greater. Inner happiness with our past overrides others' investments. It is legitimate permission to be happy now, harmonious, not just striving for power, ego or securities.

If you are part of an organisation you have to be loyal to it as you represent it. If you only have your inner self, you have to be loyal to you as you represent your inner self. Being loyal to an organisation means helping to maintain it and may require concealment, collusion and coldness for their gain. Being loyal to honesty, simplicity and kindness in your inner self, there is nothing greater or better.

We are not just a piece of kit to do one job. We are all pieces of kit and we perform various functions in different settings. We move from one setting to the next and someone takes our place like we took someone else's before. We know our place and worth but sometimes not the timing of where we are supposed to be. Sometimes we choose, sometimes others do but we are much more than what we do. We are a piece of kit for that setting but we live and love in more than just one setting.

Don't think about being happy. Just be happy. Don't analyse being happy. Just be happy. Don't give your happiness away by what others say. Don't let anyone take your happiness away by what they say.

No matter how bad things get, the quiet confidence of having the power of our teachers and ancestors and openly sharing with the young as equals is humanity.

Perhaps we need to look again and make sure we are sensitive, not uneducated or inexperienced, and just not willing or able to accept dishonest as honest or cruel as kind, being smart as coming from the heart, religion as spirituality, duty as compassion, hearing as listening, looking as seeing, thinking as understanding or doing as being.

All people problems have a process. First there is a problem, then there is an awareness followed by discussion and further thinking about it as a problem. There has to be some acceptance, and then the question of whose problem is it, who should deal with it and then letting them know. Then we can let go.

Notes From The Inside

10. Bullying

If you have a problem with bullying there are only two things you need to do. First you need to find out some facts about bullies and bullying and second, you need to come up with a management plan.

Getting through almost unbearable circumstances can leave us stronger and can be what makes us different. Some of us learn through what happens to us at school that we are different. I was in the upper sixth form and running towards a rugby pitch to play in a match for the school.

'Where are you going?' screamed the religious man three times. He said this in front of the school of five hundred boys.

'To play rugby for the first fifteen.'

The Christian Brother beckoned me over to him and when I stood in front of him, he punched me four times so hard on the jaw with his fists that each punch lifted me off my feet. I didn't say or do anything because if I defended myself, my free place at school would have gone. I would have been expelled instantly, I wouldn't have been able to complete my A-Levels and my future place at college would have gone too.

I stood there alert but somehow I detached, taking each punch to my face. I knew I had done nothing to provoke him. He had been the British Army Boxing Champion and now after the fourth punch, the Christian Brother turned his back on me and he shouted at the whole school, 'That's for nothing, now try something.'

Did his behaviour work in instilling fear in all the other school children or did he show himself to be a bully? I knew the reactions and opinions he instilled would be divided but I thought more about me because as I stood there in the aftermath of this assault, I felt isolated and alone.

My inactivity shone a light on what he was doing. Much later I learnt that when you don't know what to do, not doing anything can be the best thing and is 'masterly inactivity.'

Whatever we decide to do it must protect us first. Self-preservation is escaping into a newly discovered inner land. Initial defensive reactions to the first taste of abusive power can be answered by escalating pain or diving inside to the inner land, so we must think before acting. Sometimes it is best to do nothing. Sometimes doing nothing is a much more impressive thing to do. Masterly inactivity can have a huge impact. But also, action may need to be taken at a later time.

We may go through a lot of pain to change a difficult situation. Sometimes we need to be left alone to fight. Sometimes we need an army of support behind us.

A young boy found a cocoon and knowing what was inside it, he brought it into his house where he waited for it to open up. He waited for hours looking at the cocoon. He eventually fell asleep and woke in the morning to find a hole had appeared in the cocoon. He watched it for a long time and finally in the afternoon a black leg appeared out of a hole struggling to make the hole bigger. There was little progress by the evening and so the boy thought he would help. He went to his Granny's sewing basket where he found a delicate pair of scissors that she used for crochet work. He went back to the cocoon where the leg was still struggling to open it. He delicately cut a line along the opening and out emerged the creature.

He looked at it for a long time waiting for it to open its wings but it just seemed to wriggle about. Eventually he placed it by the open window where he thought the air would help it. He went off to ask his Granny for her help. She came back with him but the creature was lying on its back with its legs straight in the air as if dead. His Granny said, "When a butterfly is trying to get out of its cocoon, it struggles so hard that its heart beats faster and faster until its blood pressure gets very high. The very high pressure forces blood into the wings so that they open up, thus breaking open the cocoon. It is the only way a butterfly's wings can open."

The Bully

Bullying is a tool to boost self-esteem and to seem more important when underneath there is weakness. Bullies are weaker and are closer to being cowards than the ones they try and bully. They usually have fragile egos. All bullies have faults and they want to hide these by bullying someone. When their weaknesses are exposed they dislike it and stop bullying because they don't want anyone to see how weak they are. Bullies have a low pain threshold and give up because they don't like any discomfort, suffering, pain or embarrassment.

Bullies are usually bad problem solvers. Bullies are often emotionally insensitive and are arrogant and aggressive. They may have personalities we recognise and one to watch out for which is very troublesome is the 'Dark Triad Personality' combination of Psychopathy, Narcissism and Machiavellianism. Some bullies may have problems at home or have mood problems.

A bully always tries to take away your control and dominate you, so they seem in control, not you. Fighting back against a bully is fighting for you and is a serious fight. For a bully, bullying is just a game they are playing which they can give up if they experience too much discomfort or pain. To a bully, bullying can be entertainment only. They don't like being caught out or humiliated so there are ways to try and stop them which centre on their weaknesses.

Bullies have big egos but their egos are fragile. If you are being bullied, you need to understand the bully, their weakness and strengths. You need to understand the people they hang out with. You need to understand what is the bully doing it for, entertainment, boredom or power? You need to avoid being fuel feeding the bullies need. You need to know what to watch out for. Sometimes asking them to repeat their comments in front of others can defuse the bullying.

Being Bullied

Anybody can be bullied. There is no type of person who gets bullied because we can all get bullied and bullies know this. Bullies are arrogant, they want power and to be in the limelight. They can be loud. They usually pick on someone who other people like, who doesn't want to be a leader or an entertainer, who doesn't want to be the most popular person, who is quieter, happier in their own self and a kinder person and who is socially well-adjusted, without a big ego; almost the opposite of them.

Being bullied makes us think it is our fault and we are a failure. We feel shame and humiliated and we can become socially excluded. We can become depressed and we can feel like life is not worth living and become suicidal.

Getting through being bullied is not just about fighting back and standing up to the bully as this on its own usually fails. It is not just about reporting being bullied. Getting through bullying usually involves these but it is a mixture of many things and involves standing back and assessing things. Parents usually need to do this to pull out all the stops to help their child get through this.

Bullying changes our world view and can be a life changing experience. A child needs total support from parents for a very long time and almost always longer than is thought.

Bullying Management Plan

Like any unpleasant situation being bullied can only be resolved two ways, either by changing or leaving. Leaving is not usually an option although it can be.

Changing involves either changing the organisation and the bully or our self. The organisation, whether a school or a workplace, needs to be approached from the top down. They need to be approached formally as this always gets their attention. There is no point in trying to talk a teacher to help your child if they have already failed you.

The bully needs to leave you alone and if a headmaster, management or human resources point out the consequences for them, they will usually back off and stop the bullying for fear of the consequences.

Go to the headmaster and put everything you talk about in writing to send to them afterwards and ask for a response. Ask for school records as they legally have to keep school records (in the UK these are called CPOMS) which you have the right to access. If you are not happy with the response from the headmaster go to the board of governors. If they fail, you can call in social workers and say there is a child protection issue with the school.

Quite often there is only so far we can get with the school. This can be frustrating but it can also show us that it is more important to talk with the person being bullied and use our energy trying to help them.

In the workplace you need to go to the head of human resources and put in a written complaint. If you have a union, bring their representative with you. In the workplace taking time off sick with a note saying off sick due to 'Stress at work' ensures that something starts to be done about it.

Sometimes we realise the school, an organisation or a workplace do not want to change anything because their culture is one of bullying. Even though we realise that the people we are at school or work with are not 'our tribe,' sometimes it may still be better to stay and learn how to get through it.

Coping With Being Bullied

Talking about bullying with family and friends is vital to let the bullied person slowly change from being a victim to being a survivor. And it should be talked about a lot for a long time. It is not a one off conversation or a conversation over just a few weeks. The bullied person probably needs years of support.

Being angry or bearing a grudge are healthy initial reactions but these reactions need to be dropped as soon as possible as they harm the bullied person. Try and defuse the immediate reaction of anger by reeling your neck in and counting to seventeen and a half whilst you breathe slowly from your tummy.

Instead, of being angry and bearing a grudge, you need to put your energy into seeing the bully's behaviour as unacceptable. Continuing to be angry gives your energy to the bully and stops you using your energy positively for you in adjusting your attitude and not accepting the bullying. Dropping anger is a choice. It is your choice. It lets a positive reaction develop which gives you power.

You are not being bullied because there is something wrong with you. You are being bullied because the bully has something wrong with them. You will move on and do all the things you want to do in life but the bully will not and in ten or twenty years the bully will still be trying to use bullying to make them look better.

You need an enormous amount of encouragement and support rebuilding your belief that people are good. You probably need to find new friends. You need to relearn how to trust people. You need to find your confidence again. You should approach a professional who is trained to tackle bullying such as a psychologist, a counsellor, a psychotherapist, a padre or a support group. You should stick with them for a long time.

Remember that as long as you are a victim in a relationship, you cannot be the victor. You survive by relying on your inner self to guide you. The bully cannot get to your inner self. Lastly remember compassion is the tenderness which no bully, no torturer can ever remove. Compassion always starts with you being compassionate to you.

11. Torture

From 1982-1991 I saw several hundred people who had come to the UK as refugees, all of whom had survived being tortured. Their stories show us how sometimes we can adapt to cope and sometimes that the people we think are helping us are not.

I saw survivors of torture and I know many others did not survive. When I was with someone who had survived being tortured, I felt as if there was an unspoken silent trust between the other person and my own inner self. There was an unusual sense I always had which I have not described before. With each person who survived being tortured, there was a much stronger sense of their presence, the sense they had of their inner self. It was as if they didn't rely on thinking so much as their inner sense of their own self. It was a presence which I can still feel when I think of them.

Every bully and every torturer want one thing; to get to your centre and destroy it. They want to destroy what keeps you strong, your inner self. When they cannot access you by your body they turn to your mind. But by this time you have learnt that your inner harbour which has protected you and sheltered you from them, is yours and only for you to access. A torturer cannot get to you there.

We seem to have blind spots in places where we should definitely not and torture is one of those. Trust is the most difficult thing and the most important thing to restore in anyone who has been tortured.

Torture is used to display power over people in the form of another weapon against them. Torture is not used by countries to extract information from people because they know it does not work.

Because there are so few examples of looking at torture in depth, please forgive me for repeating verbatim the two examples I described in Chapter 8. First, we looked at how after the Korean War, the Americans missed identifying the fundamentals of resilience in the surviving Turkish prisoners. Second we looked at how the rest of the developed world, including the UK, copied this in taking up SERE training.

It is useful to bear these both in mind when looking at why we still believe in torturing people and why it doesn't work.

First, the Korean War again because it is one of the only examples of how some people survive torture and others don't.

At the end of the Korean War a study by the US Army Medical Corps found that of the 7,190 captured American soldiers, 38% died and over 30% collaborated with the enemy. The study concluded that the high number of American deaths in captivity and the high collaboration rate with the enemy was due to the collapse of morale resulting in the loss of allegiance to their country or to one another.

The US Army Medical Corps also found that of the third largest represented nation fighting communism, the Turkish Army, not a single Turk died in captivity and not a single Turk collaborated with the enemy. They concluded that the Turk's resilience was due to discipline, pride in their group and an unbroken chain of command. Clearly the Turks had a glue which held them together as individuals and as a group. It was more than just discipline and pride; they had powerful shared beliefs like their religion and their traditions like wrestling.

There is only so much pain we can take if someone is trying to harm us but there is no limit to the pain we can endure if we are doing it for someone else. When we are part of a group, we can endure things with more strength because we get added strength from being part of something which is bigger than us.

As we saw in the chapter on resilience, after the Korean War it was obvious that the Turkish prisoners were resilient and the American prisoners were not. Instead of finding out what made the Turkish prisoners resilient and trying to teach Americans this, the Americans came up with the "Code of the US Fighting Force," which is essentially about how to resist and evade questioning during torture. Over the years it sowed the seeds to form a specialist training known as SERE.

SERE is an acronym for Survival Escape Resistance Evasion which is a course you have to endure to be military air crew, Special Forces, MI5 or MI6. As well as the UK SERE is taught in America, Canada, Australia, and New Zealand.

Inconvenient a truth though it may be, SERE is also a standardised way of teaching people interrogation methods (how to torture others) which are prohibited under international law.

You volunteer (without giving consent) to be tortured by your colleagues who are trained experts, so you can learn how to endure it and how to do it too.

It begins with being let loose on Bodmin Moor and having to avoid being captured. When they capture you, they blindfold you and put you in the back of a truck and drive you back to the military base. You are stripped naked, and then experience genital humiliation by a blond female alongside being hosed with water. You are given no food and no sleep for days. You are made to stand at first with bright lights in your face and then made to stand hooded in darkness. You are slapped a bit but not badly beaten. Once an individual actually did escape from this. He was labelled defective and a failure. They said there was something wrong with him and he was discharged and forced to return to civilian life.

In torture the naked reality is that no pain relief is given by the military doctor or psychologist who is present. Instead they supervise the administration of pain in doses very close to death, the torture often postponed by a short rest so the military doctors and the psychologist can go for a break.

I met and listened to several people, men and women from Evin, a prsion in Iran. In Evin they sat blindfolded there usually for at least a year. Every day was the same. Sometimes food and sometimes not. Every day someone would be taken to see how much water, electricity, or other objects such as truncheons their genitals could withstand. Every two or three days the screaming was so bad it stopped and the person didn't return so their cell mates protested. Then one of the guards would come in and casually take someone's hand, break the arm or remove an eye. If ever there was bread, it was chewed many times over several days. The pieces of bread were fashioned and dried out by everyone to form kings, queens, knights, castles and pawns to play chess after they took the blindfolds off at night. I knew six people who survived. One gave me a brown solid chess piece made of bread which felt like stone. One committed suicide, another died ten years later from his wounds. The other three are here in England. Evin goes on and on.

12. Abuse

Maybe these 10 facts of responsibility could be considered alongside all religious beliefs:-

God doesn't abuse people, people do.
God doesn't give you diseases, people do.
God doesn't forget people, people do.
God doesn't choose people, people do.
God doesn't punish people, people do.
God doesn't torture people, people do.
God doesn't kill people, people do.
God doesn't poison the air, the earth, the oceans, people do.
God doesn't forgive people, people do.
Prayers don't save people, people do.

How do we let an abusive relationship continue and let abuse happen to us? What does it take to stop it, no matter what it is or who is doing it to us? Abuse does not stop unless one thing happens, we stop it. Only we can stop someone abusing us but because we have usually been programmed to accept it, stopping it might seem almost unnatural. A moment arrives when we decide to stop the chaos and trauma of the past still affecting us now and we decide to deal with it. It may be because we see clearly 'what is not resolved will be repeated' and we just don't want any more pain. Sometimes it is because we have not had much happiness. Or it can be because we see our child's eyes and see what they see.

Words tell you what is happening. Words tell you what you think is happening but the words can be the opposite of what the speaker is doing. Words can tell you what you are hearing is what you want to hear and you need to stop believing words. Greetings, kisses, flowers and gifts can reinforce that you are being treated well when these things just buffer the reality. You are being used, lied to, mistreated and abused. Words can be used to control worse than spears or bullets. Try amplifying what is really being done to you, only then will you see what is being said. Amplify what is really being said and done and you will see their control.

We can't seem to work much out. We can't stop our bullying or our torture. We can't stop our violence. We can't stop our unfairness. We can't stop our unkindness. We can't stop our thinking. We don't seem to try and stop what we can't stop. But there is a way.

The same story is heard every week by doctors and therapists. 'I was told by the religious elders my mum was not allowed to speak to me because I had accused one of them of sexual abuse. So if I don't talk it's not a problem for them, but it makes it even worse for me. My mum was told no further communication with me was possible because I was no longer one of them, as I accused them of abusing me. These people think they have protection from their God. In the name of their god they used to burn or drown anyone they didn't like by just naming them a witch.'

Taboo sounds like one of the first words men spoke to describe fear. It is a word I am passionate about because it is forbidden conversation in the corridors of power where it is simply hushed. Disapproval silences truth and screams. Its nakedness and the people who perpetuate the need for the existence of the word are clothed in infinite layers of protection. Like sex and religion it is always the powerful and the weak, the sacred and the sinful who use that word. Taboo is always bound and hidden by fear of truth.

Most people think that living in an isolated country or a small community tear down all standards as there are not enough people to check what goes on. But in the heart of London and in almost every school the same standards are identically trashed by the people who check what goes on.

Abuse is always an abuse of power. With sexual abuse it is nearly always someone you know who knows your parents too. A stepfather or mother in law, an uncle, aunt or friend will do. But if not, a teacher or a priest will appear as will a doctor, policeman or politician. It is always those in power who you believe are looking after you, caring for you like workers in homes and schools. It happens to you in secret and you are told it is your secret with them. That no one else is to know, then you are told not to lie or cry or else. Strange feelings start to grow, then thoughts, dreams and feelings go up and down anywhere and everywhere. Withdrawal, being emotional or not emotional, you know things are still wrong and have to be put right.

Their stories were similar, usually like this. "I was a child four to twelve. He was my stepfather. What shocked me as much was my mum denied it. She didn't stand by my side. She stood by his side supporting him. She wouldn't let me go to the police. Thirty years later, I had kept a journal and gave it to the police. In court other adult children appeared. Where it happened to me, it happened to them and now they have come to tell their story and see him sent down. The judge informed the court, the stories are the same. You have heard fifteen stories but there are over one hundred we know of which is average for a paedophile before they go to jail. We were too scared, too ashamed to tell."

Notes From The Inside

13. Shame

Shame is hating ourselves now for how we think our past mistakes can be seen by others. We wear shame negatively like a dirty embarrassing coat which we think others can see. If we remove and throw away the coat of shame, we can let go of guilt about our self and start to enjoy our inner happiness.

Things we do that are addictive make us feel shame and want to hide but small things we do for us make us feel good and start to melt the coat of shame we wear.

The little things we do for us can change our attitude, so we see our true self as us and not as wearing the coat of shame. This can change your life.

Victimhood is something to let go of because it lets forgiveness become a possibility. Resentment can begin to disappear and thoughts of revenge become unnecessary. Let the poor victim go and become a survivor not a victim. Focusing on your inner self, not the perpetrator of your pain, lets you heal yourself to be whole again. Meeting your perpetrator as a happy person leaves no guilt or shame in the wrong hands or heart.

What would our elderly parents say to us if they were younger and didn't depend on us? They would gently show us a reflection. The reflection would show our selflessness or selfishness, our warmth or our coldness and our greed or generosity.

We may have to say, 'Why can some people cry so easy and I can't? What stops my tears? Is it denial because I am not ready yet? Fear of what would pump them out and down my face? Blocked, stuck, not ready, fear, not enough support, no answer to them. Just being with my tears is what I want. Just being able to be with my tears is what I wait for.'

Our whole life can be based on fear of anyone discovering our shame. Accidentally revealed we have to cope with shames name. With everything we feared now named, there is nothing to fear except not disowning the coat of shame.

It could be a simple thing. It could be our name, our parents or anything in our family. It could be a little thing we do, did or didn't do but is our secret shame.

It can be where you are from. It can be you are not good enough. It can be you have failed or succeeded. It can be your friend or your family. It can be your success. It can be you have changed or not changed. It can be you have done well. It can be you are happy.

But you are not OK about you. Shame is like having a spell on you, from you. Shame is like you have branded yourself or you have given yourself a tattoo which you keep covering up. Shame stops you breaking free the spell on you which says 'Don't think, don't do, don't say, don't cry, don't even be.' Break it by accepting everything about you is OK and every little thing about you is all right. Get rid of the coat of shame, the spell, the branding, the tattoo which you keep stuck to yourself. You don't need it.

14. Chaos

Chaos can be difficult to recognise in our life because it is often a habit and sometimes a way of life. Coming from a family of chaos, discipline is at first the opposition. Slowly a frame is seen which consists of boundaries. We can begin to see we have a mind which can make choices, a body which can be strong, a heart which feels and which can accept changes. Not having to guess what comes after the next outcome allows peace to be expected.

When we can't take any more chaos it shows on our face as we are relaxed and just not interested. There's no smile from the corner of our mouth. No approval or disapproval, just no interest at all. We know it is not our way and that everyone can have their time of chaos.

We frequently hear others saying, 'Our childhood days were not like his, or hers. His childhood days were too painful to bear so he took to the drink and is still there. She was bullied so took to being in control for power.'

My childhood days were chaos and all my life I've had to work hard to look inside me to find a place to be calm. I'm still working on it to be still inside.

Living and working with others without boundaries and rules is chaos. When walls come down, everything becomes unboundaried, people, authority, power and rules. The only cure is to make rules, create boundaries and build walls so authority, discipline and identity are restored. Then there is no chaos.

Chaos is not natural because it is created by ignoring nature. Nature works by the rule of forces, always balancing, action, resting, giving and taking. Man is the only chaotic animal not working with the forces of nature. Thinking creates chaos by not balancing action with resting, not balancing giving and taking. Thinking ignores signs to stop or move. Thinking ignores where to be, ignores how to be and ignores our order. Man frequently ignores nature and order and instead chooses chaos.

When everyday life is normal, ordinariness is the usual

thing and it may seem there is little to write about it. But when things are in chaos volumes of words are written trying to understand what has happened. In ordinariness our foundations are not so clearly seen, our true self seems less interesting to record, read and see. Maybe if we wrote more about the importance of being ordinary, we would choose chaos less.

We need to think through chaos to see it more clearly. Perhaps we can say, 'I dislike chaos and sometimes feelings can seem chaotic and out of control. For example, I have passionate reactions to things which could be thoughts. These are my inner feelings about things and people which could be thoughts. I have feelings about how I am treated, where I am with someone but I don't say it.'

We may say to our self, 'It is all right.' But it is not alright to ignore our feelings. Maybe we think it is because we don't translate our feelings into words and ask for what we want. We may ask how do others seem to see it all the time and we don't? The answer is that they may have been trained to ask for what they want or they may have worked hard to express what they want.

Perhaps we can recognise our chaos and say to our self, 'I was brought up to survive chaos, I am stable enough myself but only if I have something in me which is stable and constant. It can never be you, anyone or anything or anywhere else apart from what is inside me. I have to find my own order.'

People with chaotic lives usually seem different and they may even seem more interesting as well as drawing in others for attention. But their ways are almost always self-destructive.

The human condition is an attempt to control chaos, changing it into ordered, disciplined, rational behaviour, even if it is sometimes destructive. Now chaos is something we don't understand and can't work out, so we cannot let it be what it wants to be. We need to see it but not be in it.

Chaos can seduce us. Even words can be part of chaos. Clever words can be an attempt to let the mind think it has found some sense of order from chaos when the chaos is simply due to thoughts. We may have to distance our self from our thoughts, to slow them or even stop them in order to leave us in inner peace.

Sometimes when we are brought up a child of chaos caused by others we find it difficult to break out of. It is usually because it is difficult to see the chaos and alternatives but mostly because we are creatures of habit. We can get caught in different cycles of chaos because we are creatures of habit. We stay in lives of chaos and stay in chaotic lives because we are creatures of habit. We stay in abusive relationships because we are creatures of habit. We can love and hate because we are creatures of habit. We stay addicted to things because we are creatures of habit. History repeats itself because we are creatures of habit. Habits are easier than doing new things. Most creatures seem to be ones of habits and like us they prefer habitual behaviour. Many of our behaviours become habits because being familiar with something we know makes us feel secure and feel less fear.

To deal with chaos we may also need to renew our psychological armour like a snake and grow a new skin but one that is thicker. We reach a point when we know we can't go crazy any longer because it is too crazy to be vulnerable. Thicker skinned, protecting the delicate heart within makes it more difficult to access.

When someone dies we can easily forget we have troubles of our own. Other's troubles should not eclipse our troubles. We may notice others troubles and remember them but they shouldn't take over our own and trump our own. Health trumps helping. Health trumps being therapeutic to others.

Human rights, our human right really begins with our self not wasting the opportunity we have to know our inner self first before all else.

Sometimes we must rest. Sometimes we must do nothing. Sometimes we must just be. Sometimes we should at least see this with some regularity which is an antidote to chaos. Sometimes the only answer to questions is the same. Sometimes the solution to all problems is the same. Sometimes eloquence is lost as sometimes there are no words. Sometimes in the midst of chaos there can be only one thing that is wanted and works;

nourishment with food and drink. It is basic and it breaks the chaos and is also time to rest, reflect and talk.

There are so many layers, levels, polarities and inter-relationships, but they are not necessarily chaotic. How we get to speak and hold meaningful conversations so that we do not destroy one another is maintaining some order but not perhaps done as well as some of our ancestors. The Australian Aborigines were probably the last remaining authentic hunter gatherers, partly because they were so good at it and partly perhaps because they were so isolated from everyone else that they had no-one to learn farming methods from. Contrary to how they were seen, they were highly intelligent, wise and able to communicate much better than the Europeans whose culture was imposed on them. Although they had over 700 tribal groups with more than 300 languages, they had one unifying language called 'Fingertalk' which erased all tribal language barriers.

This has still not occurred in Europe, the Americas, Africa or anywhere else in Asia. Fingertalk may have been man's greatest achievement in the creating of order and preventing chaos.

15. Letting Go

Letting go of our old self, our ego is the most difficult thing to let go of. It doesn't want to go and thinks it is really us. It makes us think it is really us when it is just a by-product of us. We can be humble and have faith in our self, not follow our thinking and let the ego be an amusement only. Eventually we begin to let go of it and see it for what it is. Then we see our thinking for what it is.

We have to let go of everything. First it's the womb, then it's our parents. The last thing we have to learn in life is to let go of life. So sometimes let go of outcomes, let go of the future, let go of thinking, let go of the past, let go of memories, let go of resentment and let go of regrets.

How often for most, if at all, can we detach from the world. Rarely someone can forget about the world and let the world forget them. Most want to stay connected, convinced the world can make them happy when all along happiness lies waiting inside.

There are intellectuals, academics, teachers, lawyers, bankers, doctors, priests, musicians, poets, singers, architects, sculptors, painters, writers, grazers, the takers, the gossipers the losers, the pretenders, those who play games and there are those who are detached, who you do not know because they just are. They have let go.

We are usually happier if we avoid trying to be surrounded by interesting people who want their sense of self-importance broadcast for a fee. We usually feel better if we avoid interesting people who seem important. It is usually better to stick with humility and the humble.

We try to determine our fate by trying to control everything we think we can but the more we try to control, the less control we see we have. The less we try to control, the less fear we have of losing control. Only then, with complete surrender do we feel secure in trusting the fate of everything.

Focusing on someone else can turn us into victims because they are getting attention which should be ours. Letting go of thinking about them frees us to be happy survivors of them, free to use our precious time for us.

Allowing others to be themselves lets us be more ourselves. Letting go of them lets us go. Stopping talking and listening more speaks to us, giving us our inner voice. Giving up control frees us because power does not give us freedom. Surrender frees us.

At some time, some stage when it is right, when we see it, when we want to, we have to let go of other people, their attachment to us, their desires for us and their demands. We have to pull back, detach and change all the connections so there is no reliance. They can be placed somewhere in our heads and hearts where we are happy for them to be, so we can be our own self. It doesn't mean we don't see them anymore; it is how we see them. They may not even know we have detached.

Look at the bigger picture of your life. See how you balance and how you try to control. Are you trying to control your work, your family life or your desires? Can you control your mind, your ego? Can you let go of this?

Looking at the bigger picture of your life. Look at the presence of balance and where it is upset. Is there balance in inner and outer life, in personal life and work life, in physical and mental life? Is there balance in what you consume, in what you eat and in your needs? Is there balance in looking after you, in listening to you and in letting go?

Why can't we let go of everything negative? Why keep it to take away the positive because it will only continue to moan and groan. We eventually have to let go of life so why is it so difficult to let go of things we don't need? We don't need approval, permission, forgiveness, success, memories, a past or a future, or to be a victim. We don't need other people's business, promises, time, chaos, lies, deception, failure, or betrayal. We don't need anger, denial, guilt, shame, fear, perfection, fear of abandonment. We need our love, happiness, simplicity, compassion and humility, detachment and boundaries to look after ourselves with patience and love.

16. Crisis

When we know we are on the edge of being overwhelmed by pain, we may decide we have had enough pain as we can't take any more. The pain may be coming from outside us or from inside us. This is when we say no to more pain and realise the pain can end. We see a way out, and then there is no choice. It is the best news we could have and is almost a time of celebration. The door has opened and denial, our soul's buffer, our minds shock absorber has gone.

In China there is no single word for our word 'crisis.' Instead there are two images. One picture is for annihilation, the other is for opportunity. We often end up right in the middle of a crisis if we have not looked at things as we could have done, and especially if we have been in denial about it. Crisis is about making a choice and it can be a transformative time when opportunities arise to change our life.

Denial protects us from looking at things because they are too awkward, too inconvenient, too embarrassing, or too painful. This is how we hang on to denial:-

We don't look at things because it is simply too early to look.

We are not ready or we can't access the support which is there.

We think there would be losses we couldn't cope with.

We don't look at things because we have not had enough pain.

We have not reached our rock bottom, been overwhelmed, brought to our knees to ask for help.

Then suddenly there is no choice because the door has opened and we let go of denial. Denial is our minds shock absorber, our soul's buffer which has gone forever. For the first time, we see we have no power over what has happened but it has stopped having power over us.

We start to think that there must be a plan which we fit into but we don't know it. We can only grow into it. Letting go of knowing un-stifles us and lets us keep growing as long as we let go. Being here in the present moment, surrendering to the future, whatever it brings, at last lets us relax. At this point we begin to feel the crisis is ending.

Happiness is our nature and searching for happiness is everyone's main desire. If we look for happiness in the outer world, after enough pain and suffering we may reach a crisis when our attitude changes and we begin to see our own happiness is located within us. There is no single formula which works best for turning inwards but whichever path we choose from the many available, once inside, all paths merge and the final path is always the same. Words cannot describe this, even these ones, but they can help turn us inwards. A crisis can be precipitated when we realise that external 'fixes' do not help us attain true happiness and fulfilment.

It may look like we are broken by wounds but the wounds can be encouraging new growth into what seems like a transformed resilient person who has all along just been waiting for the opportunity to grow.

There is a place where we are drawn to usually during a crisis, unusually in normal times, rarely all the time. But in endless chaotic turmoil no other place exists, the cave of refuge is the only place we can know. Our first and final resting place, the place which knows us best because it is our most inner self. Go to that place, the one you know as your refuge from outside, where you shine brightest in silence. You will not let your inner self down by having time and concentration until peace and happiness are uncovered once more. The cave of refuge is our harbour, safe from everything to just be our inner self.

It always helps to be direct and clear and ask yourself what do you want from you today. It is not what is usually asked but if it is not asked at the beginning it will always have to be asked at the end. It may not seem important. But it is important. Permitting a small mistake can cost us dearly because it is the denial of small mistakes which matter because the big ones are usually seen.

When we think we have chosen the wrong thing to do in our lives, sometimes we have chosen it because we need to learn from it. It may be showing us what we need to move away from or it may be shining a light on where to go. It may just be introducing us to people or places inside us where we will be happy. We do not know.

Notes From The Inside

17. Attitude

A bad attitude is like a flat tyre, you can't go anywhere until it is changed. It is not anyone else but you who needs to change. Your attitude is your inner and outer voice and is your choice belonging to no one else. Your attitude may be your last voice before everything is decided about you. You choose it. The great thing about your attitude is you are not stuck with it because you can change it, and it is only up to you. How you want to feel, what you want to say, what you choose to think, remember it is your attitude, your personal way.

How do you know your attitude needs changing? If you have doubts about your attitude or if you are not happy with it, your attitude may need looking at. If your attitude gets you into trouble, then it needs changing. If you keep on getting things wrong or if you don't seem to get along with others as you would like to, then maybe you should look at your attitude to them. It is a personal thing but you can ask others what they think about things and see if your attitude might need realigning close to theirs. Our attitude is what we would get at finishing school, if finishing schools actually existed.

Changing your attitude is your personal choice. A happy heart carrying the weight of life, a happy song sung with a lightness of heart, and a positive outlook, especially about everything is not luck but a choice.

It requires repeated work to change our attitude, but what you put in you get back many times over. Mostly it is adjusting the small things. I try and respect everyone because everyone has reasons for what they are like. I try to work out how to make a day positive whatever circumstances I find myself in because I know that my attitude influences the outcome. I repeatedly realign my attitude and say to myself, 'I will be polite to everyone. My manners will be as good as I can make them. When I am helping someone, I will be kind and I will be thankful that I am not the person I am trying to help.'

We have to face changing forces in our world just like the oceans are blown by the wind are sometimes calm, sometimes rough. Our attitude can be balanced or not and may need adjusting so the peaceful balance between opposites as our lifelong duty can be restored once again.

Our inner happiness can change our attitude to everything. The outer world can seem to be more positive, to have more meaning and make sense. But we can easily lose this sense by being too influenced by the outer world and our attitude can suddenly be changed. Our attitudes are not permanent and are there to be changed, like our bodies are by age.

When my attitude is negative, I imagine the day is a holiday or a weekend day and I imagine I am having a really good day. Oddly enough this can pull me out of a mood that has gone in to a nosedive for not very important reasons. So what we say to our self matters a lot and can change our attitude.

Our attitude to our self can let us forgive ourselves. Do we ever think about us forgiving us? Do we see us as ever being forgiven by us for what we have done or not done? We can change our attitude to what we did, why we did it and see what it showed us. Can we accept what we have done by putting our best qualities beside our faults and see that they were both necessary? We should remember that our attitude can condemn us or save us.

Your own expert on your attitude is inside you. What you don't like, what troubles you, what makes you upset; that is your best friend, your best teacher, your own professor. The best teacher is the reaction inside you, wanting you to see you may need to change your attitude to the expert on you and listen to your internal advisor, 'Professor Troubles.' Your own 'Professor Troubles' niggles your body or your mind to tell you that you may need to look at something.

There are mistaken moments when everything seems coloured with dark doom, but they are only moments. There are moments when thinking makes us believe nothing will be OK but it is not all the time. There are moments when we cannot see the meaning in anything, even us, but only for a while. There are moments when we cannot see light, when we think too much but these are moments when we only see our ego, not our happy inner self which is always there.

When you look back in your last days what will your answers be? Did you care? Was everything about you? Was it just about fun? Did you have principles? Did you have a purpose? Who were you? Did you contribute to others? Were you kind? Did you help? Were you decent? Did you change your attitude when you could?

Maybe we could ask now, what are my attitudes? Where did I get them? Do any need to change or be altered? Do they stop me being happy? How do I look at certain people, activities, places and things we can be? How do they affect others and what do they do to me? Do any need creating, adopting, cropping or dropping? If they do, I change too.

If our attitude is frozen it is difficult to be thankful. When our attitude shifts, only then can we become thankful.

Notes From The Inside

18. "Normal"

They are many clever words to describe us but they are only words not us. They are like a map, not the actual territory that the map describes. There are lots of personality types, lots of personality disorders and lots of psychiatric disorders. But again they are only words and like a map they are not the territory, they are not us, only words.

There is no normal or abnormal but basically, we can be divided into two groups. Perhaps the Second World War settled the different types of people forever. Viktor Frankl a survivor of Auschwitz frequently said in his book 'Man's Search for Meaning,' that even within the narrow boundaries of the concentration camps he found only two races of men to exist; decent ones and unprincipled ones. These were to be found in all classes, ethnicities and groups.

It is one thing to say this but it is another to have the knowledge, experience and skill to see the differences. If we can identify them we are lucky and have an advantage.

I often ask myself, 'Why can't I be normal like everyone else?' But I am told I am normal? Well if this is normal then it is pretty difficult being normal. Normal is what I would call being subject to what happens outside me as well as what happens in others as well as what happens in me. Worse is what I just sit here and imagine, fearful about the future with no place now to rest from this fearful, over thinking restless mind. Yes, this is normal.

We are not our thinking but we are what is conscious of our thinking. For all our logical thinking, for all our verbal processing and reasoning and for all our knowledge and technology, the absence of thought turns us inside and shows us our quiet still inner self.

Reality is only our best guess because there is no agreement about psychology, about religion, the origins of the universe, about physics or archaeology. We don't know what is normal. All perceptions and judgements are only our best guess. Do we imagine our influence? Maybe everything is as it is meant to be. If we change it, perhaps it is because it was meant to be changed, so maybe we only imagine our influence.

We see, hear, touch and feel our world with our senses which our brain then processes. Believing these sense organs our thinking lets us believe what our senses see is the world. But what we sense is from our perspective only and may not be what is actually there. If I look out of the window and see a blue car, I can say that the car is blue, but the other side of it which I cannot see may be pink. So it may be true from my perspective but is not actually true from another person's perspective.

Something you see from your position with your eyes is your perspective only. It is what you see, not what others see which is why we cannot in truth judge. Truth is our truth only, everyone else has their truth too. We cannot know anyone else's truth, only ours. But we could try and understand both.

Nasrudin was a legendary Mulla. Many countries claim that he was born there; Afghanistan, Iran, Turkey, India, Greece and Russia. In the Middle Ages Nasrudin tales were used to mock authority. There are many stories about him. This is about truth. One day, the Mulla Nasrudin was with the King who was trying to show off his knowledge. The king was a show-off.

'Laws make better people,' said the King.

'No. Laws do not make people better,' said Nasrudin.

'Laws do not make people more truthful.'

'I can make people practise truthfulness,' said the King boastfully hoping to impress Nasrudin.

The King built a gallows on the only bridge entering the city. The next day Nasrudin was eager to find out what the gallows were for because they looked very frightening on the bridge.

'What are the gallows for?' Nasrudin said to the king.

'Everyone who wants to come into the city will be questioned. If they tell the truth, they can enter but if they lie they will be hanged.'

Nasrudin made sure he was the first person to try and enter the City and walked towards the gallows.

'Where are you going?' asked the chief guard standing

right in front of Nasrudin so the king could see.

'I'm going to be hanged.'

'I don't believe you,' said the guard.

'If I have lied, then hang me.'

'But if we hang you for lying, we make what you said true.'

'Perhaps what you know as truth is only your truth.'

People sit in different places, postures, with different intentions, moods, problems, with different histories and different genes and although we think we are basically the same, our perspectives can be entirely different. Those who tell you how happy they are and those who tell you all the things you need to be happy too, are not usually happy.

Some situations are really difficult to work out accurately and we almost need to have an abnormal attitude to get them right. Just before I started my first shift as an emergency room doctor, the elderly consultant gave me a piece of his wisdom. 'Believe nothing anyone tells you and only half of what you see.' It has never let me down.

I feel all right even though I have difficulty not assessing things personally. This is how I see the world and this is what I have become from how I have experienced things. I can't see things so impersonally, objectively like an informed judge. I'm a bit more jumbled up by life and sometimes I don't come out perfectly right. I'm all right but I'm not always all right. I wasn't made perfectly but that too is sometimes all right. I frequently ask myself, 'Can I be more like everyone else, more normal. Can I stand back not judging? Can I be quiet when I could speak? Can I just let things be? Could this sometimes be me?'

Can you be more integrated, more well-rounded, like everyone else, or are you pretty much stuck with what you are with your faults? Can you have different attitudes at the same time? Can you hold more than one view, seeing things more than one way? Can you be objective and personal as well as be clear and imaginative? Can you read everything just visually and see everything in terms of words as well? Can you hear with your vision and listen with your eyes? Can you integrate different attitudes, perceptions and judgements, be conscious of them all, then that too with compassion? It is all possible.

Sometimes it is good to abandon what we think we should be. Giving up all attempts to be normal is freedom from other people's rules. Giving up norms is finding our own normality which is what we value above all else.

In days of great peace nothing happens. In the stillness of days of great peace there is just the peace of stillness. When a struggle is finished, like a dark distant storm we know there is only temporary effortlessness because life cannot be still as change is its nature.

No wants, not wanting anything is the best barometer of happiness. Isn't it strange how only through solitude you learn how to be with others, only through silence you learn how to communicate, only through stillness you learn how to move, only through being you know.

19. The Importance of Being Weird

I used to seem strange to me. At first it used to worry me but not anymore. Yes, I don't feel so much part of the world as others seem to. They seem so involved, it almost makes me dizzy. I try and stay away from business, happier on my own being quiet and still, even though I know this is not possible much of the time. Not so concerned with building things up for the future, I'm most myself getting on with the task at hand, especially if there isn't one. It is my world. You have your own world too. All you have to do is see it, and it is yours. Unknown to you at first, a brief encounter with your inner self can lead to the point of your life.

Do you often feel as if things are a bit vague, that you are in a strange state, different from others? Do you feel as if you are different, moulded in different ways in ways you cannot say? Join me and others in being weird but happy in what we are. Whoever said it was not good to be weird doesn't know it is good to feel weird, to think weird, to see weird, to be weird. Being the odd one out, you eventually see there are a lot of odd ones out, lots of us. So many that the only conclusion is the ones who are not odd are the odd ones. Crazy people are often much more sane than we know and the apparently sane are often much more disturbed than we realise.

In my late twenties several things made me quickly decide I did not want to be a psychiatrist. This was the first one. I was in charge of a psychiatric day hospital mainly for patients who had been discharged from the main psychiatric hospital after an average stay of 2-3 months. Most of the patients were not well enough yet to be unsupported at home. Some of them had trouble in seeing themselves as normal and saw themselves as stigmatised. The annual hospital fete was happening in two weeks and the patients and staff decided to go as the Lewis Carroll's Alice in Wonderland's 'Mad Hatters Tea Party.'

Everyone volunteered, including all the patients and staff. We made our own costumes to take part in the small parade at the fete and compete with themes from all the other departments such as administration, rehabilitation, short and long stay wards, nursing staff and many others. We were applauded the most and everyone respected our stance in trying to destigmatise mental illness. We were clearly the outright winners.

The winners were chosen by a very traditional psychoanalyst. When the winners were announced we were excluded on the grounds of poor taste. The patients and the staff at the day hospital celebrated all afternoon because we were so happy to have got away with being so obviously different, untraditional. We were true to our selves.

Next time you look at someone and label them as a fool or an idiot, perhaps you should question how superior your thinking and judgement are to theirs. Have you seen how thinking can be our greatest enemy and the fool has chosen to daydream and watch the stars at night instead. Next time you look at someone and see them as a fool ask why are they smiling and you are not. Ask why they are happy and you are not, then consider if they have chosen wisely and you not.

Do you get a sense of eeriness more than others? Does it make you feel connected in ways we can't describe? Does the sense of eeriness around you stay when you think it has gone? Is it with you at night when you sleep? I thought it was just me but everyone seems to get this. Everyone I've asked thinks they would seem abnormal to others if they mentioned it. Perhaps being more open about it would normalise eeriness.

Some people always seem to be standing back, not at the front, not eager to engage but watching from a distance. They don't expend armies of energy participating in events of the world. They just run their own life of enjoying the present moment. They are watchful, always seeming stationary, waiting for change, even though they don't move. We are different, so are they.

When some bulbs we plant are different and do not flower, when some trees are different and do not bear fruit, do we blame the sun? When someone lets us down, when we behave badly, we should not blame but accept this is who we all are.

Imperfection, taking risks, making mistakes and getting it all wrong are not like landmines trying to destroy you but only there to annoy you and encourage progress. Taking risks, leaving forgiveness behind, exploring what is not allowed, encourages further exploration. Perfection is the enemy of progress because it stifles looking further. Perfection halts all growth. Progress with imperfection is the growth process so let yourself be wrong.

They will always wonder about the crazy one because he or she is the one with the cutting edge, the one with the crazy unreasonable truths they are too scared to explore. For example, it is good to wander into your enemies' territory where you are treated with respect and willing to learn what they have to teach you about yourself. You can leave more free of what they think of you, more free of what you think of them.

I can't watch drama on television. I can't watch most plays. I can't read complicated, involved novels because what people don't match up to is what I see every day. Reading, theatre, television remind me of my job with people, so forgive me if the way I relax is to stay in my own world. It is just my own way.

What made me quit psychiatry was the treatment of a survivor of Auschwitz who had a problem with a chronic low mood. When electro-convulsive therapy failed, it was suggested at the weekly meeting of all the psychiatrists that she should have a frontal lobotomy. My objection on the grounds that psychotherapy should be continued as she had had enough torture was ridiculed, as was I. After I left, I was reassured on hearing research evidence that for people with severe psychiatric disorders, a six week stay in a South Indian temple doing light duties produced the same improvement as a month of standard psychiatric treatment.

What if this path doesn't go home but leads to other places including happiness, suffering and then dying alone? Accepting what are not usual routes is what we are. We can be open, seeking, sometimes just being still with our adventures warming the heart.

Divine inspiration is supposed to be regarded as the

only thing that logic cannot challenge or argue with. If you write from the heart of your inner self and if you follow Advaita Vedanta then your inner self is God, so your writing is divinely inspired. In Christianity where the Kingdom of Heaven is said to be within, then god is inside you, so if you write from your heart it can be divinely inspired. I haven't got as far as looking at other religions because it seems if you can see it is true for one and you understand it is true, and then the truth the divine is you.

    I started off being regarded as sensible by the establishment, and then I refused to agree to conditions of living which to me were like killing myself, so I walked and walked until I was far away. One day I was shocked when someone told me I was the establishment. Shocked, I asked myself how did this happen? I had walked so far away from the establishment that I could see my own happiness without all the attachments, because I was detached.

    Do you fill in spare time with activities which make you happy because you are not happy? Do you do things you know are second rate to being happy because you know you are not happy? Sometimes it can be best to look for what our happiness is inside us, not as an activity. I value by sight but not above all else, not above consciousness. Sight is not consciousness, nor is hearing or doing. Consciousness is life.

20. Being Positive

I was sitting in a small one-roomed bank in South India, sweltering at 40 degrees. I was waiting for the only employee, the manager, to serve me. He sat at a desk beside a cast iron safe. He called me to sit in front of his desk and asked me how I was. I didn't know what to say but then I saw it. There was a sign above him on the wall behind saying, "It is nice to be important but it is more important to be nice." He was being kind, nice, and gentle and I appreciated this.

You may be the best at something but one day someone will emerge who is as good as you but only one of you will succeed. The only difference may be that they or you are nice. Being nice may be the only quality which defines you differently. Being nice is simple because being nice is uncomplicated unlike being important. Being nice is being considerate about yourself in how you use yourself with others. Being nice may be why you are happy, have friends and are loved when someone else is not.

When you do something to help someone it makes you feel better. If it made you feel worse you would stop doing it, so do help others but know it is for you. Not long ago the wealthy used to be benefactors to artists, writers and the poor to ensure they could survive. Not anymore. Today, encouraged by the tax-man to pay less tax, they give donations to charitable organisations which have pension funds, investments and CEOs. Perhaps we could personally go back to where it started; service, yes a servant to something needy, not to be advertised or monetised. Only anonymous volunteers allowed to do the work, no paid workers taking money from a pension fund built on widow's donations, who go without food and heat. No chairman or chairwoman, director of fund raising or director of human resources. Come and help if you can show up anonymously in your own time.

There is a silent ghost of service. She arrives unannounced at any time in your life when you can only look back or while you still have time. She wants to know about anonymous service only. How much of your time here did you devote to quietly helping animals, people or plants, their world, the world of the sky and the sea? The only things counted when she lets you look inside you are silent anonymous service.

You might want to look at this because you may not want one of your last thoughts to be, 'I wish I hadn't been so negative but more positive.' With no knowledge of when that will be or if you will have that moment to reflect, it may be wise to start being positive now.

Wonder can be a gift and a curse. To wonder about the stars can open the soul or stop the mind. Wondering about wonder is both. Inner peace is melting away the negative, the positive outlook reinforced. But there is a side to it that can be anxious vigilance which drains efforts to be positive in outlook.

Isn't it great that darkness can be removed? Isn't it great? Isn't it great that happiness follows suffering? Isn't it great? Isn't it great that happiness is inside? Isn't it great? Isn't it great that anyone can be happy? Isn't it great? Isn't it great that it is free? Isn't it great?

It is not the beauty in the light of a sunset, the contours of the mountains or in the rivers of the earth but in us where beauty is. Beauty is inside behind the eye, expressed with a smile and always inside. Shared beauty takes us further inside to our own light.

Identify and concentrate on your wish. Say what you want and how you want it assertively to yourself, and then simply say it to others too. Only then is your wish possible. The past was like a comic book cartoon of a dark cloud following me everywhere, darkening what could have been brighter moods, until I decided to use it. I decided to look at it, to write about it then to sing inside me. 'It's going to get brighter. I'm gonna fight you with happiness and light.' I sing about it out loud when I walk and deliberately skip a step. The cartoon dark cloud now winks at me from a distance as it looks around for other victims.

How can anything be as welcome as the early morning sun? How can we be more grateful than for the early morning sun? How can anything make us more alive than the early morning sun? How can anything make us happier than the early morning sun? There are only so many sunrises you can see so it is good to go out and see as many as you can.

Today's good news is that I woke up, so did my wife and daughter and our cat. The good news is we talked on the way to school about unimportant things. The good news is I have the day off and I'm going shopping. The good news is I will take them somewhere to just be still. The good news is we return after just being still.

It is possible to write about things other than happiness but why write about things which we don't want. It is better to write about what we want, what we can't see and how to get them rather than to look at what we don't want. It is equally important to read, discuss and see what stops us being happy and what helps us be happy. There is no point in reading, discussing and seeing what makes us unhappy. It will only make us more unhappy.

A smile can change your whole day, more than words in a book, more than a week off. A smile can contain what we find difficult to say. Some days a smile can be what we most remember and we find our self saying 'At least I made someone smile today: a five year old girl and a four year old boy, a woman with no money to pay for her pills and a man with not enough patience.' A smile when passing someone who has no connection with you or interest in you, apart from giving you a smile, can't be bought. A smile from a much older or younger person who you pass by may be the best smile you ever get, that stranger's smile you can't forget. Why is that particular smile so important? Maybe it is like a mirror reflecting an inner sedated part of us we love but can't express. Maybe that smile is our known but hidden potential inside. Us in full bloom spread fully open like full consciousness. Smiling may even make us live longer but that is not why we should smile. We should smile because we feel more alive today.

You can keep drinking bitterness and keep chewing on resentment, searching for hooks to hang them on, trying to find a person to say you are right but they will stop you feeling better. Or you can dodge the negative getting in your light, keeping it to the side of you, so you can see your light. Make sure you get things out of your light so you can shine bright.

Thought is a gift but it also creates our ignorance. Consciousness is what we are, not thought. So get out of your way. Get out of your own light so your inner self can just be and shine bright.

How often do we decide to do nothing when we have nothing to do and are not tired? How often do we decide not to think and just be still? Do we ever experience being still? Do we ever stop and just be still?

What we think we sense and know, perhaps we imagine much more than we would like to. What we can sense and know is only visible if an inner light is turned on. The inner light can only be turned on by turning around, looking inwards not outwards. The things of the world become secondary, and then they too become brighter.

When you acknowledge you are hurt and want to stop it, you need to understand why someone did it so you can stop hurting, forgive them and move on. You have to understand them but understanding may be left up to you. It can exhaust us beyond a point, so we have to accept our forgiveness may be limited. Listening to your inner self, keeping the ego in check in stillness, the inner person is heard. Listening to your inner self is the greatest kindness you can receive.

What am I bringing to the table, to the relationship, to the problem to solve it, to life to make me happy? We can only bring our self. Whichever way you can see it, it doesn't matter as seeing, hearing and feeling are only pointing back from where they came from, inside.

I remember, so can you, clear sunny days, everything bathed in sunlight, everyone bathed in sunlight. Is there any difference in anything, everyone or the sunlight or is it the way it is seen?

It is up to you to feel better, to look inside and ask your inner self for the help you need. This is where I start.

Unaided I stand before you asking for help and protection. Mercifully hear and answer me. Only here inside in the stillness is the help, the protection, the kindness and love.

Whether or not we admit it, we all live by a set of rules. To live well and be happy we need to ask if these are our own rules, or are they someone else's rules. I write my own rules down, check them and reflect to see if I still feel OK about them and if they need adjusting. Writing them down makes you clearer about you. Cringe-worthy though they may seem, here are my own rules.

To be happy, spend as much time as you can being still, as it will keep you on the path you are on. Call it anything, meditation, special time, and realise it is always with you. Be a weirdo, be odd, be abnormal, don't fit in, fit out. Be yourself, kind with compassion. Keep everything simple and smile at yourself. My rules sometimes work for me. Everyone else's sometimes work for them. Be firm and flexible and aim for happiness. Don't waste time wanting to get to some stage of your life faster as some things can't be controlled, especially when you are old.

Eat fewer root vegetables because they concentrate chemicals. Eat just enough. Eat more fruit, nothing processed. Walk slowly, ride and drive slowly, think slowly and smile when you can. Go barefoot or have good shoes and don't forget to sleep in the open as well as in a good bed. You spend most time in both. Spend as much time outside as possible but don't sunbathe. Walking is the best exercise but don't do anything dangerous unless you have to. If you do, don't do it without crash landing gear and when it is over smile. Don't see sad films, read sad books or listen to sad music.

Treat others with the manners a servant would show to a King or Queen, then everyone is respected. Only see good friends, don't use them or pay them. Stick with positive people not negative people and return other people's smiles. Be as wrong as right but don't take daily matters into the night and give your smile whenever there is a chance. Thinking is not your master only your friend. Your master is not your ego which you see as yourself but instead it is your inner self. Happiness is the single aim of your life. Show your smile.

Notes From The Inside

21. Acceptance

When we are in a painful place, sometimes it seems there is no way out. It seems there is no alternative but to wait and accept it. In accepting that we can't change things, this acceptance changes us. Only then do we see things differently.

Whatever the day brings I try hard to accept it because it has been given and it has to be lived through, even if it has been given just to reject. I am thankful to difficulties. Yes, I thank them. I don't have to be ungrateful, resentful or envious. But being thankful cures it of any negativity and helps accept difficult times. There is always a way out of every situation. Even accepting being blocked may be the only way out, once it is accepted. When it seems there is no way out, it can be the only way.

Thanking the cause of our distress seems like an error of thinking. Being grateful may not be what we think it is but the opposite. Yes, maybe it seems like an error of thinking to thank the cause of our distress but thinking can be wrong. If so, then we can rely and trust on a part of us that comes before thinking. Just have a go and try it once. See if it works. See if your attitude seems changed if you thank those who seem responsible for what happened to you. Did it eventually bring you to a better place?

Did they unintentionally help to eventually bring you to a better place? Try saying thank you inside. You never have to say it to them, only to be thankful for them, otherwise it may not have happened. We can welcome what has been given to us.
Saying thank you for this, even if it seems painful, changes it into a gift like nothing else can and shows us the positive hidden in us. Being thankful shows us lessons only learnt one way. It shows us understanding other ways. Being thankful lets us grow in ways we didn't know. It lets us move on when we are stuck. It releases us when we feel trapped. It shows us how to move on to the next stage. Being thankful turns our mistakes into opportunities, our losses into gains, our problems into solutions and shows us we can fix what is broken. It shows us how to

make the past good in the future. We should be thankful for what someone has given us and sometimes for what they have not given us.

We can't change what was given by nature but we can change how we nurture it. We can't change what has passed but we can change our attitude to it. We can't change another person but we can accept them.

We think we will change. We think things will change and improve, not knowing, like a flower, which can't become anything but a flower, we also can't become anything other than what we are. We can only be what we are.

Why should we be frightened of loss or of dying or death? It is nature and fate letting us fulfil our purpose. They cannot be changed from what they are letting us be; what we are. Suffering is not an option because it is handed to you on a plate as a dish which you have to eat. There is no choice about receiving it but there is a choice about acceptance. Suffering breaks a part of you down again if that part has not been properly rebuilt since the last suffering. It is suffering's nature to help us, as is your nature to be your inner self, which is happiness.

The true meaning even if spelt out and illustrated is not accepted. Instead euphemisms, metaphors, mysteries and stories are nearly always preferred to truth.

We can think a lot about many things, of others and where we are but at some stage we see we have to embrace it, so we need to find acceptance. Acceptance is not just taking what is offered but welcoming what is offered as a gift. We need to be thankful. The harder it is to accept the more welcome it should be. Acceptance is not just about receiving but also discovering inside us what we need to accept.

We don't get the chance to rehearse how to respond to bad news but just in case, here are what we most commonly go through; acceptance, acceptance and more acceptance. This is usually preceded by shock, denial and nausea, then anger and disappointment.

We look for all sorts of reasons for why we are like this, our parents, our country, our school and our town but it cannot be worked out. We think we are limping; disabled. We think we need support and help but sometimes we cannot be worked out, only accepted for what we are by us.

Accepting what comes with age is a slow thing not a shock. I know my memory is a little bit worse than two years ago. Once or twice a week I can't remember some words but because I am immersed and don't value them, I let them go. Not having to build up any more, being able to let go, accepting the state I have always been in is only present for me now.

It is only now nearly at the end of my work that at last I think and feel able to do it. Unfortunately, a tiredness has entered me simply from the wear and tear. Earlier on the journey of work seemed easy and smooth and we had to accept that this is what we had to do. Later we have to accept that we have to stop doing it.

The amount you can do and the amount you want to do reaches a peak, then irreversible decline begins. There may be productive times with great effort but gone is the leisurely brush of the hand. There is little time left, less willingness of the brain cells to work together. Everything of value has already been gathered in, so the hand is more desperate. But then it relaxes as we see it is the same hand which helps acceptance.

Just now the sun disappeared below the horizon but it is still very light and dusk will be here soon. Acceptance of this inevitable darkness makes me turn up the light inside me. With one sunset or a hundred years of them are we wiser, happier, fulfilled or are we the same as we were with the first one? Perhaps acceptance of today, your inner self and someone is your most important quality.

My notes to me about my faults are so many only a few can be mentioned. Like having a short fuse, being bad tempered, getting angry and raising my voice, perfectionism, having expectations of others and me, not liking criticism, not taking orders, other's forgetfulness, not being reciprocal, being thick skinned, frustration at being too soft, not able to reel my neck in, being wrong, being sad, being sentimental and being too self-critical. Maybe you can see why we are the most difficult person we ever have to work with.

    We have to pick ourselves up and carry on in whatever form we find we have become. We may not see we have the desired resources but find we have the determination to find them. We can't stop the inner self. I obey its commands simply because seeing what the world is like, I just surrendered because there is no choice as surrendering is a choice-less path. I gave up trying to fight writing as it is too strong for me, so I obey its need to be expressed. There is only one time I am able to stop it and completely ignore all writing, if it comes from the mind not the heart.

22. Keeping Our Balance

Maintaining our inner and outer balance is always happening. We are always trying to be healthy not unhealthy. We are always trying to be happy and not be unhappy. We try to be more conscious of our thoughts taking us over, but we are not often successful because they are so powerful. Maintaining our balance is not always automatic and can take most of our energy.

The last time we saw Jim he was saying goodbye from outside his ex-government owned house beside Glastonbury Tor. He lived on the lower slopes of the Tor, so that he could be on an upward mountain path. He brushed aside his fatal condition and showed himself, right to the end, as a person who was both true to himself and knew himself.

The last time I saw Jim on my own, he was waiting for death to arrive, meditating upright in the middle of a hospital bed. There was a sense of everything being perfect with not one thing wrong. I wanted to sing aloud to him the chant of the sacred mountain we had both visited. But without saying a single word, instead, we silently sung the same internal song. Old friend your body has gone, but I see we will not be forgotten for ignoring our thinking, because our silence quietly sings on as we walk up the sacred mountain path.

In some ways we are all on our own inner mountain path. When you seem down and have fallen over, get up where you fall, even if you can only crawl for half a step. Mountains don't let you leap up their side; they give you a choice to let you slowly grow inside. Every wrong path you take, every mistake you seem to make are all progress on the inner mountain path. Whilst you camp on the inner mountain path, sometimes clinging, sometimes singing, every pause, when there seems to be no change, are growths of inner silent strength. Our growth is not what it seems. It is mainly within, unseen because it is becoming conscious of what we already are.

Keeping thoughts away is not what we are used to doing. Saying no to thought is not what we are taught. But when we see thoughts cause most misery, we start keeping them away to make us happy.

Our performance at being still reflects our ambition, which reflects our hunger, our desire for happiness. When you know stillness there is nothing to say about it. Nothing can make it clearer than being still. Have you tried being full of emptiness so you are fully empty? What a sense of joy when no egos are in a crowded room. Thoughts pushed away, compassion is to all and stillness reigns. No matter how long we live or where we live, we have to surrender to that stillness within.

I remember a birthday meal I spent in a supermarket car-park in a car on my own, eating delicious food in my car. The next birthday I sat in another car park of that chain of supermarkets. Then I thought I won't be here tomorrow because with my travelling work done, I will be at home, not in a car park of a strange town I once lived in, but where I live with homemade food and homemade love.

Being away what is missed the most is not the surroundings, your things but the company of those you trust, those people. The conversations which take you on a journey are only because everyone knows you for who you are. No one is trying to impress you, only stick with you until they have to go. It is where we all want to be again, back with those, back in that group, back on our own with them.

To be happy is everyone's desire because it is what we spend all our time trying to be. We try so many different ways in all sorts of permutations. There are some who are lucky and realise we are happy just with what we have today and we don't need anything else. Do not underestimate the skill required to ignore the negative in life to make you happy. It takes up most of your life.

It is our choice what we have. In the room we choose to live in, our responsibility is to change it if we want. There is nothing wrong with desiring what is natural. Happiness is our natural state. No one can be criticised for being happy being their self, except if it harms them or others. Eventually we know we can't be happier or more grateful than we are. Our inner territory cannot be guessed. We can have an opinion about it.

We can read about it and think we know it or we can surrender, serve it and be it.

Living attached to others, it can be impossible to be in solitude. Living detached you can be in solitude but be with all people if you choose. If you mix with people you can become like them or they may become like you. You can choose to be with certain people but don't forget how you are influenced is your choice, not theirs.

So many people stay together because of what is in the basket; the material things in their life. The basket itself is not worth anything; its only value is what we have put into it. They only stay together because of what's in the basket. Sometimes the basket becomes more important than all the reasons they joined together. Restoring the balance is crucial.

When you are taking but in disguise of giving, don't try and make it look like someone doesn't want what you are offering. Be honest. If you want something; ask for it. If you don't want something; say so. If you want to exchange; say it. If you are happy; share it. Only buy what you like, what you need, what you want. Don't buy to have something because of its value to others. It will only make you unhappy.

How can anything else apart from madness truly understand madness? How can anything else apart from sadness truly explain sadness? How can anything else apart from having lived truly understand life? How can anything else apart from mourning truly understand mourning? How can anything else apart from receiving truly understand giving? How can anything else apart from being loved truly understand love?

Why are we so complicated, full of things that don't necessarily sit together easily? Let me speak for me first. I look for inner peace yet at the same time I seem critical of injustice. I am detached from most people but passionate about anyone's loss of rights. I sometimes protect the defenceless even if it results in the offender suffering from seeing what they tried to impose on the defenceless.

Not everything that is wrong can be made right because they are the same; only on the other side. Right and wrong like light and dark need each other to exist, like men and women who can only exist because of the other.

We are known for our possession of things, especially money, power and ego. We are known less for our non-attachment to things and especially our simplicity, humility and compassion.

23. Suicide

Suicide is frequently in the news and it is good that it is talked about more openly so we can help to prevent it happening. However, we do not talk about the relatives and friends left behind when someone has died by suicide. Doctors spend a lot of their working time talking with people who are depressed hoping to help them improve and not get to a point where they die by suicide. It is difficult to notice successful suicide prevention but not when suicide happens.

I always remember the first patient I was looking after who died by suicide. As professionals we never forget them, so how much harder is it for the family? Perhaps this shows the difficulty in coming to terms with suicide and the difficulty in helping someone who is left behind.

The priest listened to the desperate mother talking about her son who died after jumping from a multi-storey car-park three weeks before.

'I know he's in Hell. I've lost him'

'How do you know your son is in hell?'

'Because that's what happens if you commit suicide. You know, there is no other place. So you go to Hell for eternity.'

'But what if after he jumped whilst he was actually falling, he changed his mind as many do? What if he decided he no longer wanted to commit suicide, then he would not have died with suicidal intention so he would be in Heaven. This can be non-suicidal death.'

The mother started to change her mind about her son by a simple 'what if.' Perhaps we should not just assume someone thought a particular way. It might be wise to discuss it with others before we make a conclusion.

Two months later the woman came to see me about her fear.

'I saw the priest about my son who died three months ago. He said my son might not be in Hell because he may have changed his mind in the last moments before he died and decided that he wanted to live. I heard what he said and if it's true then my son could be in Heaven, but I just can't be sure if this is what happened to my son. I know I can't be sure but I just need convincing; and I don't know how.'

'You could write all this down in a letter to your son and say how you feel. You could tell him about your pain, that you want to know what happened. You could tell him you worry about him and tell him how angry you feel and how sad you feel. Try and say all the things you have not been able to say to him. Take your time writing it and then post the letter to yourself with a second class stamp, so it takes a few days to get to you. When you get the letter addressed to you, sit down and write the reply you believe he would send back to you.'

When we have unfinished business about someone who was taken suddenly from us without any warning by an illness, an accident, or suicide, we can find it difficult to get a sense of moving forward. We can feel frustrated and angry as it seems there will never be any kind of closure. Writing the letter, posting it and then writing the other person's reply to you can help heal that wound.

We often take too much responsibility for another person's suicide. We use the three guilty terms, 'I could have, I should have, I would have,' or 'I coulda, woulda, shoulda.' If someone is determined they are going to do it, nothing anyone can do will stop them. We are nearly always left not fully understanding what they were thinking. Sometimes it helps to come to a point where we accept that we will never know any more. Sometimes only with this acceptance of not knowing we can move on with our own life.

But sometimes suicide is not always what it seems and we may be given misleading information. More soldiers committed suicide after the Vietnam War than were killed in the war. Male American war veterans who die by a single shot from a gun are still registered as accidental death whilst cleaning their weapon, never as suicide. Suicide is not what it seems as male American war veterans who die in a single vehicle car crash on their own are still registered as accidental death, never as suicide. In America suicide is not what it seems because if you've had enough, if you point a plastic gun at someone, the police will usually unintentionally ensure 'Suicide by Cop.'

Notes From The Inside

24. Anger - The 3 R's

We are always up against it, difficult people trying to get us in the ring, trying to engage us to psychologically spar with them, but it only disturbs your peace. So many times we find ourselves sparring and before we know it, we have been lured into the ring. Try and remember your inner happiness is what you are, then your guard is easier to keep up.

Most people will get in the psychological boxing ring and have an argument with you, even if you don't know them. Because we fall for it so easily, we have to be more on our guard, so just don't get in the ring. If you don't get in the ring you won't get psychologically mugged and you will begin to feel better, so don't get in the ring.

Start by saying to the other person, 'You are right.' then keep on saying, 'You are right, You are right,' which will defuse the situation. Just don't get in the ring.

You need to reel your neck to stop pointing your chin at the other person. Reeling the neck in lets you think and see what the other person is seeing and thinking because of your impact on them. To reel your neck in may need sensitivity and education to show you how to stop being provoked into impulsive responses and instead seeing and aligning with the honour of your own kind.

Three R's to remember are: Don't get in the Ring. Reel you neck in. Say to yourself and the other person You are Right, and keep saying You are Right.

I can see how wrong I am being irritated but not at the time it happens. How do I bring that time from being reflective to being present at the time? The answer is to notice it quicker each time.

Anger can rapidly grow into violence because of lack of the experience, training and skill to express an alternative opinion in a more constructive way.

Anger is not always a weapon used against someone. It can be self-harm, a weapon against yourself. Anger is feelings which are drunk because of not halting them with the mind.

Embarrassing the mind with its wildness, anger jeopardises all other thoughts and colours the picture we give others about us when the true picture is unfinished.

My thoughts may be different and are different but we are the same. How could anything be otherwise? We share the same time here and respect is how we all work together under the same sky. So we all need to keep trying.

Almost at the end, why is it we look back? Is it to make sure we are happy and not regret or maybe both? The emotions are more present than ever as time goes on. The only way to keep them under control is to give them a quiet voice but, never not heard, never not felt, so they are always understood.

Forgiving and apologising are never forgetting. They mean always remembering so we don't make the same mistake. Apologising often assumes more understanding than may be possible. Accepting an apology often assumes more understanding than may be possible.

Occasionally you have to let yourself feel bad for a while without letting it last too long. Sometimes you have to feel how bad it has got and only then you decide to change it. If you don't experience pain you cannot experience the alternative.

25. Kindness

What people are and what they do does not make as big an impression on us as how they make us feel. One of the most popular quotes about kindness is attributed to the novelist Henry James: "Three things in human life are important: the first is to be kind; the second is to be kind; and the third is to be kind."

When was someone last kind to you for no apparent reason? Did you feel better in some way, happier?

We have an inner wealth we can give away which doesn't cost us anything at all. It makes us better to give our self to other people, so find a way to give away your inner wealth. Be extravagant with humility, then you may become intoxicated with inner peace. Kindness with simple disciplined good manners and respect make us feel better and civilised. I don't want a gold star experience of anything without authenticity.

It's the smallest things we do which tell someone everything that needs to be known, confirming we mean what we are. It can be the handmade card, the x for kiss or smiley face at the end. Looking you straight in the eye tells you it's not a lie. A cup of tea can be enough, waving an extra goodbye on that day without a tear in the eye. It's the smallest things that we do which tell someone everything like a smile.

Gentleness and kindness are not our first reactions to many things. Instead defensive actions are more automatic, thinking they are saving us from our mutual aggressive destructiveness. Kindness is a better reaction but is easily faked by those who want to use us and can leave us distrustful and fearful of kindness itself. But kindness can change our view of the world. How we feel and what we do. Being kind is the most important and also the most civilised way we can be, but we forget this.

Our failures and our faults have the most important function, more valuable than our success and strengths. Our failures and faults keep us in check circling success and strengths and show us how to be humble.

I remember a woman I worked with. She kept to

herself and none of the things which she quite liked in shops or magazines ever found their way into her life because when it could be kept secret she gave everything she could away. A life full of happiness, passed without incident, without a flicker of notice. She was here then gone but perhaps she is waiting to be found in you.

We should say hello on the street, yes because it is polite but most of all because it is friendly and it is kind but it might also have unknown consequences. Maybe we don't see any opportunities to be kind each day. Passing someone is one of them because even if there is no reply, you may have stopped their train of thought which might make them change their mind.

Our jobs, clubs and class do not define us or sculpt our choice to make us decent. The clothes we wear are not badges of honour. If you are conscious of your inner self you cannot be false. If you think, write, speak and act for your inner self you cannot be false. Our inner self cannot be taken away by those with no principles, even though they torture us. It is the smallest things we do for our inner self, the secret treat of a tea in a café in solitude or when we listen for a long time to a lonely stranger. Connecting our self with others in solitude, in solidarity, is our best human quality.

26. Expectations

When I was twelve years old a much older cousin visited us on his way back from Biafra. He was a priest who was also a magician and a member of the Magic Circle. He taught me less than a handful of simple tricks, two of which I rehearsed and perfected. I am not a magician. I realised this when some of my magic tricks didn't work when I showed them to some friends. I felt embarrassed and I also decided there was no point in carrying on just being a fake. I know I can't entertain partly due to lack of confidence because also I don't see myself as amusing. I realised then that I am not an amusement but instead I am happiest being my own self. Perhaps I was a bit hard on myself and maybe I was better than I thought. I learnt there were some things I was good at and others I was not very good at. My boyhood fantasies of being a good magician ended quite quickly as I learnt to try and have more realistic expectations of myself. I had chosen to put a pressure on myself which I didn't need to and eventually dropped it. It made me more cautious.

You don't have to have expectations. Having no expectations takes a lot of pressure off you. You are not open to disappointment but more open to being surprised. Having no expectations closes a door on a source of negativity in your life. You are also less at the mercy of others and probably more in control or your happiness.

Being thankful for what we have instead of wanting more is not the first step in being present; it is the only step in being happy now. We are not taught how to be happy without expectations of other people. We forget that we already have happiness.

Those who expect nothing are usually disappointed. Those who have nothing can lose it when they get something. Perhaps it is better to stick with what actually is.

Sometimes we lose sight of our destiny. Immersion in the vast sea of our apparent interconnectedness in family or in work can easily drown us, so we are overwhelmed and can no longer be detached. We get drawn in, lured in and tempted. It is better to be a brief visitor like a holiday maker on vacation, detached from destinations but not from our present destiny.

Can we look at and drop our expectations to let our children be whatever they are no matter what. Can we not impose our thoughts hopes and dreams on our children? We can only help them with the tools to do whatever they are going to do. Sometimes we can only show them how to be still, to have the strength to endure life.

I trust me as I can't pretend I trust anyone because anyone can let you down, even if they don't intend to. You can be set up to compete without knowing that you are competing but you cannot set yourself up. That is why you should trust you even if it seems you could be wrong.

27. Grief, Adjusting to Death

The loss which comes with death can be like finding yourself in a powerful river where you have no control except to keep afloat just to breathe. This is where I was taken. I wrote it down for my daughter who was only seven years old at the time.

"He's gone," my aunt said. There was a long pause . . .

I held the phone to my ear and felt the silence of the aftermath; the moment after the announcement of death. This was immediately followed by a sense of solemnity.

My mind, frozen and numb in shock just let the body take over. A gnawing physical emptiness in my stomach appeared.

"We'll be on the first plane over and see you later this afternoon," I said. It was ten o'clock on a Saturday morning. My uncle had died just a few minutes before in hospital aged 83.

I then told Chrisie my wife and India my daughter. We all said some things which are now forgotten. Life seemed to be put on hold and it all appeared hazy and blurred for a while.

I wanted some time on my own so I walked upstairs to be alone in the front bedroom overlooking the River Severn, looking west towards Ireland where he had been born and where he had also died. From the bedroom window I was looking out at the estuary of the River Severn, the large crack like an open mouth, between south Wales and England, probably visible from the Moon.

As I looked over the river going out to sea, I thought of his spirit rising up, leaving Ireland, leaving this world. 'Goodbye, goodbye old friend, now to become an ancestor. Goodbye . . . forever.' There was a reluctance to cry, to let the tears come. It wasn't time.

Again I felt the discomfort in my stomach. The pain reminded me of the loss which I had first felt just after my father died thirty years before, then last felt ten years ago when my mother died. But this wasn't so overwhelming. It was the same quality; just a lot less intense.

I stood looking out of the window into imagined faraway places down the river. Easily visible to the North across the Severn lay Wales, whilst England lay to the South. The large bedroom window also overlooked the shutdown Berkeley Reactors 1 and 11 which stood up like windowless monoliths just half a mile away, having formed the first commercial nuclear power station in the world until they were shut down.

He had worked on them both with the construction company Taylor Woodrow as a Senior Electrical engineer in 1959. I thought how just like the power station, he too was now switched off. Berkeley 1 and 11 had ceased operation in 1979 and he left to go back to Ireland in 1999 after a career as a civil engineer. He went back to retire and die and in 2009 he had just more than the ten years there he predicted.

As a boy he had won a scholarship to Nathy's boarding school in Ballaghaderreen in the west of Ireland but had contracted TB and had to return to live at home in his sixth form. So he didn't go to university; something which was unfortunate for him because he was particularly bright. He could quote a lot of Shakespeare and do calculus; the latter a subject which held no interest for me because I believed it was both beyond my grasp and well . . . not interesting. He then excelled at Gaelic football playing for his home town and county. After school he left Ireland and spent all his time in England.

I had last seen him three months before. He was always a large man, blue eyes with silver hair swept back revealing a broad forehead. He was tall and broad with a very positive attitude. He was good natured with a twinkle in his eye. He had been through enough to always want to see the good in people. He had a soft spot for my daughter and my wife and we were fond of him. Our parents were all dead and because he was the last of that generation, we regarded him as the elder of the tribe; the person with insight and wisdom. He was my mother's older brother and had married my aunt in his forties. I knew him better than my three other Irish uncles and we got on well. One of us always had a glint in the eye about how good life could be. We were positive about life and always glad to hear from each other.

So just a few minutes after the call, the three of us had

already psychologically left our home and we were heading to Ireland. An hour after the call we were at Birmingham Airport on the forty five minute no frills budget flight to Knock Airport in county Sligo in the west of Ireland. The forty five minute hire car drive from Knock took us to be with Brendan's widow in Ballina.

Whatever you are doing after a death; for some days it seems you are really in a choice-less automatic state of mourning. It is almost like being hungry all the time but you can only be in that state and no other. People may come and go; so might you in that you go here and there but you are in that altered automatic state . . . which does pass. It slowly diminishes when you start doing your normal duties again. That's how it is with me.

The meeting and outpouring of empathy and compassion between bereaved ones can never be described in words, so I'll leave it there. But there was something very special to me that I will share with you that I had never experienced before and not even heard described; so I'll try and tell you as best as I can . . .

We returned to the funeral home in the evening and the body, what was left of Brendan, had been brought up from the hospital in Galway to the undertakers and had already been dressed and coffinised.

Brendan looked like his father had looked when he was dead. Horizontal, still and pale with a slightly Roman almost hooked nose. I'll probably look like that when I'm dead, I thought . . . if I don't die with traumatic wounds to the face. My thoughts covered over the things I couldn't say to myself or to him.

Jim, my aunt's brother arrived. He had a two inch long dark brown beard and long dark brown hair. Jim listened carefully to the funeral director as he was given instructions for the gravediggers.

It seemed that because Brendan was a large man the funeral director was making sure that the grave was going to be big enough for the coffin.

"Tell the grave digger it's got to be three wide, eight long and five deep. Make sure now it's five feet. It has to be that. If it's for a double grave to include your sister here in the future, it must be at least five feet deep." She didn't seem to mind being reminded of her own future death. But what is there to be surprised about; only that we are surprised by it when we shouldn't be.

"Got it. Five feet deep," Jim answered. I had never heard instructions given to someone to pass on to grave diggers before. But these were someone's last vital statistics and they had to be right.

"That's the crucial one to remember. Can't be taking his coffin out to dig deeper years later."

"Got it," repeated Jim.

Jim had listened and repeated it to us as we walked out.

"I've got it. Five feet deep," he said to his sister. As if it would help him remember the numbers to pass on to the grave digger.

"Five feet deep," he said to me too, as if I should remember it in case he forgot it.

The next morning I felt like a week had passed. There were brief chats with people I knew and people I didn't know, at the house, on the way to the newsagent, on the phone and everywhere I went. There were condolences and warm wishes and remembrances from people about Brendan. But we had to get on with the business of moving towards the funeral and burial.

In the afternoon I had to go and meet Jim to check the gravediggers had the right measurements for the grave. The graveyard was several miles out of town and I assumed that because the grave diggers were independent of the funeral home, we had to double check they got the size of the grave right. India had been particularly close to her great Uncle Brendan as she had never met any of her grandparents. Not knowing your grandparents is one of the problems children have when their parents are older than other parents; like me. I was consciously and deliberately taking her to the graveyard because I thought visiting the site where he was going to be buried would soften the sight of seeing Brendan's coffin being taken from the church to the graveyard and being lowered into his grave. I thought it would help her move on. I also thought it would probably be good for me too.

For a child there is nothing worse than being treated like you don't actually know what is going on when you know full well what it going on, and sometimes better than the adults.

On our way to the graveyard I remembered a young woman came to see me who had alcoholic parents. Her parents ignored the fact that her grandmother was seriously ill and actually dying. When she was thirteen she spent all her spare time looking after her grandmother and just being with her. When she became very unwell, the girl told her alcoholic parents but they ignored her. She told them her grandmother needed to go to hospital but they ignored her so she called an ambulance and went to the hospital with her grandmother. She called her parents to say her grandmother was dying but they just said she would be OK. She died after just a few hours. When she died she was the only person with her. After the funeral, when they all got back to the house, the girl was told to go outside and play in the garden whilst her parents and relatives ate and drank inside. Now as a young woman, she needed to talk through her parent's behaviour but also, what she did needed acknowledgement.

Because of hearing of experiences like this, I thought that if my daughter, who was only seven years old, was more involved in her great uncle's funeral that she might cope better.

Brendan had mentioned a couple of times to me that he had a plot where he and his wife were going to be buried, but I hadn't really ever given it a second thought. But now I was driving along narrow Irish country lanes doing circles trying to find the plot in Cloughan's graveyard which was apparently easy to find because it had an old run down church in it. I was told the old church was easy to spot as it had no roof, only the sides and gable end walls. I followed several signs and eventually came upon a building fitting this description in the distance. Opposite the graveyard was the old church. I looked out for Jim, but couldn't see him. I had the sense that this area was not just rural but very isolated. I could hear and feel the wind. The view was stunning. In the distance was a lake and behind it a conical mountain like a volcano. It was peaceful.

I parked the small hire car and India then walked into the graveyard with me following her. She wandered around the graves happily whilst I wandered around looking at some of the memories carved on the gravestones. On a baby's grave I read "Those are not stars in the sky but portals though which our little ones watch over us." I thought of how much a child means to us and how much we mean to them. I thought about all my ancestors and I knew India was thinking about them too. I was happy for her to be wandering around the graveyard looking at the graves because I knew from my own childhood experiences of walking in cemeteries that they were a time of happiness for me.

I was wandering around the graves and was thrown back to when I used to walk back home from St Mary's Infant's school in Ipswich. I remember most the serenity of walking amongst the long dead. On winter afternoons I would walk down a long lane, alongside the outside wall of the graveyard as the gates were locked with chains and padlocks. It was a thirty minute walk and there was only one street lamp at a grass triangle where the lane turned left down a hill leading to Tuddenham Road where street lights re-appeared. I remembered a gate at the bottom on the left which was locked in the winter. But the dark never scared me. I too was six or seven then. It was the old graveyard in Ipswich.

But during spring and summer afternoons on the way home from infants school, when it was not so dark and spooky, the gates of the cemetery were open and I walked on the path on the other side of the six foot high green metal fence, inside the graveyard following the same route as the lane and the six foot high green metal fence. At the end of the path were some steep winding steps leading down to the end of the lane and the gate was open.

There was all the time in the world without any pressure to look at all the weeds, wild flowers and lichen on all the old graves. Usually I would go wandering and look at the names and the dates on the graves. It was something adults didn't talk about so I was discovering the world of the dead for myself. These people didn't try and tell me what to do, to control me or do me any harm. They weren't enemies or bad in any way. They were almost like friends, letting me just be. I came to see these walks by the cemetery as times of freedom and serenity.

It was freedom from school and home. The walks through the graveyard were some of my peak moments as a child. It was how the world was to me then, a place of stillness and calm in the middle of a turbulent childhood. At either end of the graveyard were adults; at school giving instructions, commands, tasks and at the other end parents strained by their own turbulent childhoods. This was the first thing I had found to do to escape from them both. And now at the newly discovered Cloughan's I still had the same sense. My seven year old daughter was the same age I was then.

We must have wandered around for twenty minutes looking at names and the ages of all those buried there when I heard the engine of a vehicle. I raised my head to see that it was a pick-up truck trying to get in the graveyard. The driver had got out to open the cemetery gates.

In the distance, across a couple of stone walls, I could see a large bright yellow digger which was used to dig the graves. I walked with India over to the pick-up truck which was now purposefully driving across the graveyard towards us. It stopped and I recognised Jim.

"How ye?" he said, lowering the driver's window so he could lean his elbow on the open window frame. Jim looked a bit dishevelled, his hair everywhere a mess, like his clothes. It seemed to me that he had probably come straight from his farm because he had brought the pickup truck with his tools in the back.

"Good," I said. India smiled at him and I noticed there was a car behind him with Jonny, Brendan's other brother in law at the wheel. His son Declan who was maybe twenty sat beside him. "Couldn't find the plot," I said.

"I'll show you. Follow me." So we walked slowly beside

the pick-up truck as it turned left and stopped half way along the bottom row of graves. I noticed then that Cloughan's was only about a quarter full as it had plenty of empty space for new graves. There could be at least another twenty rows I thought.

Jim got out of the pickup truck and I scratched my head as to why he had stopped here.

"Here," Jim said. Jonny and Declan had now got out of their car. I looked at them and at Jim as he looked head bowed looking at the ground. I must have looked bewildered because I felt it.

"Where's the plot?" I asked Jim, who looked up at my eyes for the answer. He was silent but he nodded to himself and looked down at the grass around our feet. There was no awkwardness just a solemn silence with respect for the grassy spot.

Jim broke the strange silence and spoke first. "If the first turf's not struck within two days, they say its bad luck and it'll soon be turned again. Let's measure it and get the turf off first."

"What do you mean?" I asked. Jim looked down at the ground in front of us.

"It's a belief that if you don't dig the grave within two days, someone else will die."

I noticed there was a pick axe, a sledgehammer and other tools in the back of Jim's pick-up. I suddenly saw there were also several shovels and spades which made me feel the rush of adrenaline in my stomach followed by a slight race in my heart rate. I was surprised by what I realised but not anxious or fearful in any way. My mind was open to what it was about to experience because there was no other way of dealing with my own and my young daughter's predicament.

There were no grave diggers. We were going to dig the grave ourselves. The yellow digger in the distance was only for the locals who were too old to or who no longer went along with the tradition of digging the graves of your relatives. I looked beside me to see if India had realised what was happening.

"So, let's make a start," Jim said looking directly at me. As I bent down to whisper in India's ear.

"We are going to dig Uncle Brendan's grave," I said
"Yes, he will be so happy."

Her answer surprised me and made me realise how completely normal it must be for a child to think the family should perform the last duties such as digging the hole in the ground for the body; but as a society we do not. We have accepted the programming that we should distance ourselves from any close contact with most of the aspects of the dead. We have become observers attending a funeral, not participants in our final ritual and have given up part of the grieving process. We were about to experience physically and emotionally all of the forgotten realities of digging a grave for someone you love.

I remembered seeing a man who had chronic difficulty maintaining relationships with women. He appeared to find it difficult to speak about his mother and to connect with any feelings about her.

He had been kept away from every aspect of his mother's death. The only thing he could remember about the death of his mother was when he heard it announced from the church pulpit on a Sunday morning. He wasn't allowed to go to the funeral and he wasn't even told where his mother was buried.

He acknowledged that he had never had a chance to say goodbye to his mother and he felt blocked and confused about her. Eventually he came up with and talked through his plans which involved finding out where his mother's grave was. He then planned to have his own ceremony there to say goodbye to her.

On the day he chose to find her grave, he dressed in his best clothes and went to the graveyard alone. He took a letter he wrote which he read out aloud to her over her grave. It was a long letter saying everything he had missed saying to her as her son who was left behind. He planted some daffodil bulbs and then had some picnic food he had prepared. Before he left the grave he set off some fireworks. When I saw him a few a weeks after, his sadness had gone. He had a lightness in his face and in his eyes. He had completed his part in his mother's funeral and worked through his unexpressed grief.

The five of us, Jim, Jonny, Declan, India and me stood there for a few seconds looking down at the imaginary boundary of the grave plot.

"Eight by three," Jim said as he measured out eight feet by three feet with a simple tape measure. He marked off the four corners with four tent pegs and one piece of string. I was in a state of bewilderment because I had never seen a grave dug before.

"Here take this spade," Jonny said, handing me a spade from the truck. He then grabbed three shovels from the truck to give to me. With my hands full I ended up giving one to India which she passed on to Declan, who put it down on the grass. India held on to her shovel. We were now a team with a single job to get done together; to dig Brendan's grave.

Then Jim started clearing the rubbish off the grass, scraping it with the front of the spade. His spade stopped at something which I bent over and picked up.

"It's a flat squashed tin of lager. Looks like it's been run over by a steam roller,' I said.

"Well, well," Jim said as he took it from me and laughed.

"He was more of a Guinness man," Jonny added. Everyone laughed and it was the release of tension through black humour which we all needed to actually begin, get stuck in and start digging Brendan's grave.

I had been bewildered by everything so far and I must have seemed as if I was in a daze. I couldn't find any comfort zone, or anywhere in me which felt normal about digging Brendan's grave because this was not normal. I only felt strange because it was entirely new.

No one had actually talked about digging Brendan's grave or hinted at it or used any euphemism. Perhaps digging your loved one's graves was respected and viewed as being too solemn to be given any words.

I could only remember very vaguely as a child hearing about how some old families in the west of Ireland dug the graves themselves and buried their own. My aunt's family was one such family and my mother's family had also done this a long time ago. We were all doing this right now. Digging the graves of your family is an ancient practice of the people of the extreme west of Ireland. There had been no chatter or idle talk about it. It was approached in a reverent silence with respect for the dead . . . to a point.

I knew India would be coping much better with digging her great Uncle Brendan's grave because she knew no different. But when I reconsidered this, I thought that she would find it odd as well because no-one had ever mentioned digging a grave to her. But there again why should a child find another new thing in their lives any more surprising than any of the other new things they come across. I had never met anyone who had ever dug a grave and still haven't.

"Are you OK? I mean OK about digging Brendan's grave?"

"Yes." She beamed a happy smile to me which told me she was good with it all. I wandered several times around the outskirts of the very shallow hole left by the absent turf. I helped to clear the little bit of turf which Jim had managed to dig up. The turf was about three to four inches thick.

India, Jonny and Declan similarly busied themselves with dealing with the turf skimmed from the top of the grave plot. Within 10 minutes it looked like a very good shallow outline for a grave with a foot high mound of turf piled up at the head end. As Jim seemed to be the person who knew most about what we were all doing, if not the only person who knew what we were doing, I thought I would ask him about what we were actually doing.

"Do many families dig the graves like this?" I asked.

"Not so many these days. Maybe one in ten I guess." Apart from being a farmer, Jim was also the singer and mandolin player in a local band. He was a fit man.

"Have you done this many times?"

"Eleven now," he said starting to break the earth. I could see beads of sweat breaking out on his forehead.

"Here let me have a dig." I took the spade and proceeded to dig into the earth.

At first the earth was cold, damp and heavy, but quickly it seemed to have changed. I noticed it began to have a warmth to it just like good cloth does. It was the final thing which would cover Brendan. It was like I was preparing his clothes. It became a warm thing to be doing, not a cold exercises of shovelling earth. Just as an expectant parent prepares a crib to welcome the newborn baby, so I was preparing the earth to welcome Brendan back. This sense of welcoming extended to the mountain, the lake, to the rest of Ireland, the sky and the sea. I had never experienced this before and I wondered if it was because I was actually in the grave, with the soil, aware of how it can envelope us that I had this new sense of its importance. Here the live earth welcoming back its own was nakedly real.

I noticed there were a few stones, but not too heavy for the spade to lift up. I dug with the spade for about five minutes and when there was so much loose earth that there was nowhere else for me to stand but for me to stand on it and compress it I switched to the shovel to lift the loose earth out of the grave.

Twenty shovels later and the beads of sweat from my own forehead had formed thick drops of sweat which fell onto the lenses of my glasses. I had trouble seeing through the blurred sweat covered lenses. I wiped them with my shirt and saw India watching Jim and Jonny and Declan looking at me. At first I had appeared fit and strong but now I was just at the end of my strength. Five more shovels and even when I wiped my glasses, I couldn't see through the blurriness of the sweat on my lenses because now they were also misting from the heat from my head. So I had to stop. But I stopped mainly because I was exhausted.

India was handing mints around which Jonny had given her and she was eating them like they would all be soon gone. I felt and saw Jim use a bottle to tap the side of my upper arm which was holding the shovel.

"Have a drink," he said.

"Couldn't think of a better drink," I said drinking a mouthful. The ice cold liquid hit my tongue, the inside of my cheeks, the roof of my mouth and when the coolness hit my gullet, then my stomach, it jolted me into full consciousness. I gulped down three more mouthfuls and felt my thirst was quenched and the sugar entering my blood stream. I felt a little dizzy from the rush of the sudden entry of water and sugar into my system. We all stood and passed around the bottle in a social moment where it was time to share any words we had in our hearts or minds.

"When I dug the first couple of graves, we didn't have bottles of lemonade. My uncles and brothers had bottles of whisky and by the end of it, if you hadn't actually fallen into the grave; you were ready to lay in the grave and go to sleep," Jim said, smiling and taking a good look at the state of me, already soiled with the earth.

"I feel like that already," I said. As I wiped fresh soil off the bottom of my trouser legs.

Out of nowhere, I felt a stillness standing in the middle of all of these graves. Here with my family the stillness reminded me of the stillness I felt on those walks through the graveyard in Ipswich when I was six or seven. There was silence as everyone rested and there was a great peace within me. It felt like it was for a few minutes or maybe it was the stillness always here inside me.

"It's a lot more work than you would think," Jim said. I was proud of the work I had done as I had managed to take Jim's four inches of turf down by about nine inches; so we had done one foot in half an hour.

"So how long do you think it will take us to do the next four feet?" I enthusiastically and rather confidently asked Jim; thinking he would say maybe an hour to an hour and a half.

"Four to five hours if we are lucky"

"You've got to be kidding. Are you serious?"

"It'll take that long at least."

"Why four to five hours. I mean we lifted out a foot in half an hour."

"What you've been up to so far shovelling is the easy layer on the top compared with the rest."

"I'm interested now."

"Well the rest comes with ever increasing pain. When you are in a hole four feet deep there are two sources of massive effort." Jim looked at the others then at me.

We all went quiet as Jim began to dig. After fifteen minutes he handed the spade over to me. But after only ten minutes digging, I handed it over to Jonny and I then had a rest for five minutes.

I was standing in the grave where Brendan's feet would rest in the coffin. I stood silent but I felt I was almost thinking aloud . . . 'So this is where he will end up for eternity or until the world goes dark as the sun goes out or it is destroyed by a comet or whatever.'

"Odd to think this is where he will be forever,' Jim said, almost reading my mind.

"Yes for all time. Maybe thousands of years," I replied.

"But he would have chosen this spot because it looks over the lake to the mountain."

"Some say the best spot in the West."

"It's strange that we spend a lot of time getting everything ready for a new born baby to arrive into a happy home. We spend a lot of time helping someone to get ready to be married but we don't do much for when someone dies apart from make arrangements. This is so different. It is complete involvement; complete immersion, literally in the actual ground."

"A great reminder of our own short time here too," Jim added.

I noticed we were all doing a lot of looking down at the ground then looking up at the sky. It was as if each of us was trying to work something out, reconcile something, and see some link between the earth and the heavens. I noticed we each did it in an almost compulsive way every once in a while. It was a new body language as if we had to emotionally compensate for the immersion in the feminine mother earth. There was an acceptance of her welcoming back the return of one of her own. But maybe this intense immersion, actually in the earth, needed to be compensated for by looking at the opposite; the great spirit of the sky. Perhaps this body language I saw was simply about restoring inner balance in this traditional ritual.

When I got my breath back from all the talking and thinking, I realised I had been standing for a while looking at the mountain. I used the shovel to move the earth which we had all shifted away from the edge of the grave. Jonny handed the spade over to Declan. Declan was the fittest and dug for fifteen minutes. Finally India was given the spade and also dug. She dug with the same enthusiasm as everyone.

This went on in cycles of passing the spade and shovels around in a very well organised manner. But we slowed down as the hole got deeper and had breaks every fifteen minutes for lemonade and mints. Eventually curiosity as to why Jim was so sure about his four to five hour estimate got the better of me.

"There can't be any big surprises," I said.

"See that long handled shovel." Jim pointed to the tools on the ground. "The handle is six foot long and it only has a small shovel blade so that when you are in a four foot deep hole, you can still lift it up above your head. You have to lift it up two feet above your head to seven or eight feet from the bottom of the hole to get the dirt out. You can only lift a little at a time."

"Yes I can see now just how that can get more difficult. So what's the second source of massive effort?"

"That." Jim first pointed to the mountain in the distance, then to the sledgehammer.

"I don't get it. The mountain and the sledge hammer. What do you mean?"

"We have a lot of that mountain in here." Pointing to the mountain again, "And we have to use that," pointing down to the sledgehammer. Jim handed me the spade again as it was probably my third time to dig but when I dug I was stopped abruptly by a solid mass of something. Jim heard the noise, saw my face and pointed to the mountain again. Now I knew what he meant.

"Granite. Solid granite boulders."

"How do you know?

"I've dug in this graveyard and it's the same every time. You are OK for the first three feet then you hit this layer of boulders which cover the whole of the ground at that level. It looks like an hour and a half job getting the soil out but you can't lift these boulders out. You have to break them up with a sledgehammer. You'll see."

The cycles of digging continued around the boulder which was in the centre of the plot at about three and a half feet. Another one appeared at the foot of the plot and then another at the side of the plot. The one in the right hand side wall of the grave eased out with some effort, fell on the floor, then couldn't be moved. So we had about a foot and a half of dirt to clear and three boulders which we couldn't even move. This is where the pickaxe came into its own.

We dug around them and under them and got down on our hands and knees to clear as much soil as possible and then the tough work started. We didn't even try to lift them out.

We stopped for another rest, leaning on shovels and pickaxes. Jim picked up the sledgehammer and leant on its thick handle.

"Lincoln was a grave digger," Jim said.

"Abraham Lincoln?"

"Yes he was a sexton in a church in Indiana. You know someone who looks after the buildings and the land including the graves."

"Never knew that," I said.

"Tall too. Six foot three. When he was shot, he was taken to a house across the road from the theatre in a coma. He was too tall for the bed so he had to lie diagonally. Lay like that for nine hours in a coma before he died. Grave robbers tried to steal his body for a ransom but they got caught. They opened his grave in 1901 and took a photo of him. You never know when you are last going to be disturbed but no one's going to be interested in the likes of us. We will lay in peace. I'll bet Lincoln never had to use a sledge hammer in the graves he dug."

Then Jim started chipping away at one of the big rocks which was two foot long and a foot wide.

"Five minutes is all I can do," I said, once more with sweat pouring off my forehead and down the lenses of my glasses. "I feel like a convict breaking rocks" I added. But five minutes was the same for each of us with an extra heavy sledgehammer. It was as much as any of us could do. Only one of every five hits at a granite stone would yield a chip off the stone. So it was painfully slow.

"Now. Let's get rid of the rocks," Jim said. It was an announcement that the boulders were finally broken up small enough for us to carry.

"All pieces of stone have to be lifted out of the hole, put on the side and then we get rid of them. When we start the next dig, we don't want to have to lift all the stone out again. We'll carry them over to the stone wall over there and dump them over the other side."

Down at the end of the slope where future rows of graves would be dug was the stone wall. No carrying device was available so we each cupped our hands full of bits of broken of rock.

After forty minutes of removing the broken up rock the biggest chunk of broken rock had to somehow be lifted out. It could only be lifted by three men. It had to be lifted four feet up to the edge of the hole which was now nearly a grave. Once out it was easy to move and Jonny and Declan then rolled it down the gentle slope with their feet to the three foot high stone wall. They then they lifted it over the wall, dropped it on the newly broken pieces of stone and the small heaps of dead flowers from recent funerals.

"We need to straighten up the walls a bit," Jim said.

"You've got a keen eye, so give it a go." Jim continued looking at me with a questioning expression.

"I'll give it a shot," I said kneeling down before sitting on my bottom then sliding down into the grave. This was deep now, I thought. Since my last turn of digging, the others had flattened the bottom out at about five feet. My mind started to wander . . . 'I've never been in a grave before and the next one I will probably be in will most likely be my own; if I am buried.'

I wanted to complete the task but I also wanted to get out of the grave because well, it was not mine. Graves are a place you don't want to be. There is a taboo like being in someone's secret place without them knowing. I hope you are happy here Brendan, I thought. Peace at last. No more work.'

I used the larger shovel to scrape off earth from the sides, so the walls were more vertical but I was alarmed at just how much new earth I was filling up the grave with as it was going to be really hard work to lift it up at least seven feet with the long shovel. My mind went back to the most recent tomb I had visited in The Orkney . . . the Tomb of the Eagles.

The tomb which is over 5,000 years old and under 10 metres long has to be entered by lying on a trolley on four wheels, which was like a large modified skate board. You have to lie on your back and pull the trolley along by a rope which is attached to the ceiling of the tunnel lined by massive stones. Pulling yourself on a trolley by a rope makes you realize that the only reason you can't just climb through is because the walls are several metres thick.

In the Tomb of the Eagles they found the remains of 342 people. It is believed that the bodies were left on slabs of stone at the entrance to the tomb, and when they had been picked bare by white tailed sea eagles, they were then interred further inside the tomb. It is thought that this allowed grieving time. Essentially, a body was put out of sight when the person was no longer in living memory. They had changed from relatives to ancestors. Perhaps it was their way of coping with the loss of loved ones. I thought how digging this grave was allowing us to move on with the grief process. Then I realised I was thinking about all of this whilst I still digging, so I stopped for a moment.

"Shall I keep going Jim?"

"Yes. It needs to be a little broader at the bottom so it's square all the way down. Don't worry about the earth. There are enough of us to get it all out."

"I was feeling a bit guilty about that."

"Don't worry. It's the easy bit now. It will make it look all square."

"Right then." I attacked the wall for the last time with the shovel and did the finesse work on the top bottom and sides.

"Can I help Daddy?" India said loudly

"Of course. Hop in." I was surprised she wanted to join me in the grave but she probably heard this was the part that made it look good.

"It's nearly done isn't it?"

"Yes, nearly there."

"It's the last bit like icing a cake."

"Yes. I suppose it is." India had given me a sense that this ritual task was coming to a close. I knew I would probably never do this again. I scrambled up the sides of the corner of the foot of the grave and sat on the corner looking at India. She was busy digging.

"Look daddy look daddy look!" she said. "Look . . . daddy. Gold!" I looked down and saw she had picked up a small rock about two inches wide by three inches long. It was glistening. I thought I was seeing things for a moment. "It's gold. Gold!" India said. I looked at her and her face was smiling brilliantly.

"Gold," she said. I looked over to Jim who was smiling.

"It's gold alright," Jim said

"Gold, Gold," India said even more excited

"Fool's gold," Jim said.

"Who is fool?" India asked.

"It's named that way because it's actually a type of silica, like the stuff sand is made of."

"Oh," said India disappointed. "I would have had to put it back to be with Brendan even it was real gold," she added. "It's not mine anyway . . . it's the Earth's."

I thought about this and replied, "Just like the fool's gold is the earth's, so is Brendan. And so are we. We all have to be returned to where we came from. We only leave what we have shown others about ourselves." I was left thinking about memories we leave in others people's minds and ones which vanish with us and my thinking wandered off looking at this . . .

When my mind had stopped wandering I came back to the present . . . It now looks like a grave. It is a grave, I thought. This is the interior of Brendan's grave. It's a good grave. Not just a hole. But a hole made with care and some precision to welcome his coffin. Others will dig this out again to bury his wife when she is dead. They won't have such a hard job as us breaking up and lifting all those rocks out. They will hit the top of his coffin with their spade and stop dead in the realisation that it's his coffin. Will I be there? Will any of us who are here now be there? I noticed India looking happy at her work smoothing the ground, the part where his head would rest.

"Great work," I said

"I'm making a comfy pillow for his head." She stood back and paused, looking at her work. Then she looked up at me. "Done Daddy."

"I'll lift you up and out,' I said and I jumped into the grave and knelt down. India climbed onto my knee then used my shoulder to lift herself up over the edge and onto the ground above the grave. Jim held her hand and steadied her as she stood upright. I carried on smoothing the floor of the foot of the grave. I didn't notice India being lowered down by Jim and re-joining me. I was thinking to myself . . . A grave is the place a man stays the longest. The longest lasting structure he will be in.

There's been no solemnity. No one has been sad, miserable or morbid. It's been a strange task the main aim to make a good grave for Brendan. If anyone had any guilt bothering them when a person dies, then digging their grave would probably completely absolve them of it. I had no guilt but I was looking back at my time with Brendan. I thought of my mother and their three brothers. Brendan was the last.

I was jolted out of my dissociated state by a gentle slap on the back. "Ok, you're done," said Jim. I had been standing in the grave with a thousand yard stare thinking to myself with India smoothing out the floor of the grave in what seemed like loving small strokes. This was wonderful closure for her but also for me. It had given us sacred time that cannot be had elsewhere or in any other way.

After four hours the lemonade ran out and so did the mints. Both had been a good source of energy. Four and a half hours after we had cut the turf the grave was ready. We were exhausted, covered in soil with wet clothes due to the perspiration.

"Here, give us your hand,' Jim said.

"Ok," I said, feeling my feet on the bottom of this grave for the last time. I leant back against the wall behind me and put my right foot in the wall in front and leapt forwards and upwards as Jim's arm lifted me up in one powerful joint manoeuvre. As I stood there Brendan now seemed like he was already a long way out to sea just as if he was in a Viking long boat which was about to disappear over the horizon.

There was now a perfectly symmetrical rectangular hole, eight by three by five feet with mostly flat walls and a flat bottom. There was a large mound of earth to the left which looked as if it came from three holes this size. Jim said that this could be shovelled back in fifteen minutes.

Half an hour later we were back at my aunt's house where she greeted us smiling.

"All done," I said to my aunt. India was proudly smiling.

"You're both covered in soil. Did the two of you help?" she asked

"Help. The two of them dug at least half of it," Jim said.

"And you too India?"

"Yes. It's a really nice grave." My aunt had a happy smile for India. She walked over to her and hugged her.

"You are such an angel. He would be so proud of you."

The next thing to do was to get cleaned up and then go straight away to the funeral home to meet and greet everyone who came to pay their respects to Brendan in his coffin. This was the modern version of a wake. I found myself thinking about how modern man now has a form of body disposal known as direct commitment or more simply direct disposal. Once the death certificate and cremation form are signed by doctors, the body is taken straight to a crematorium for disposal. There is no service and no mourners.

I sat with my aunt, Chrisie and India in a row of chairs facing the coffin which was open. The door opened at six and nonstop until eight o'clock, people briefly paused in front of us shaking all our hands, saying what were their last words about him. Most seemed dressed in their Sunday best but some had come in straight from their farms, from manual work and were in their working clothes. I didn't count the hundreds because after the first hundred handshakes, all concentration was lost apart from being polite, solemn and maintaining eye to eye contact. I heard many things said. Not the same thing was said to any of us. Each one treated us differently. Most went up to the coffin first, leant over and kissed his hands and said something quietly to him. The last of hundreds of people went through the doors two hours after we started shaking their hands. There were a few lovely humorous things said and some very serious religious things as well. But most wanted to comfort us in their own personal way.

They were showing us we were part of a community, a family, which was their family. I must have seemed strange to everyone because I felt dissociated from what was going on. Yesterday morning we had all been at home. Now India and I had dug his grave and here we were with Chrisie and my aunt and Brendan for the last time, now prepared for the next day. I wondered if he had any regrets. Then I thought would I have any and my mind wandered . . . I was making my own list of last regrets and trying to let go of them.

The next day we stood waiting outside the funeral home for the body to be placed in the hearse. We were to make the three minute walk behind the slowly moving hearse across the River Moy to Ballina Cathedral for the funeral service. As soon as the hearse started moving, my aunt, Chrisie, India and myself were about to take the first step as the main family group behind the hearse when suddenly, India let out the most distressing cry of grief I have ever heard. It had such huge emotional power that everyone stopped for the three or four seconds until she had finished. Most including me had never heard such a shrill of emotional power.

A few minutes later we walked into Ballina Cathedral and we took our family seats at the front. The organ filled the air with sweet sombre music as the coffin was carried slowly up the isle to the altar. As my uncle passed me by in his coffin, tears began to flow and I could not even see the coffin. But then my eyes dried and I could see clearly for the first time in a long while.

One year later. After a night staying at a friend's house on the lower slopes of Ireland's most sacred mountain, Crough Patrick, we decided that on our last day in the west of Ireland we would go and visit my Uncle Brendan's grave in Cloughan's cemetery. We were not alone because there was for the third year a gathering in the abandoned church before dawn at six o'clock. I was no stranger to this graveyard because only recently, in terms of the age of the burial site I had dug his grave with my daughter and other relatives. But it was now too early in the morning so too dark to see anything else other than shadows of stone walls against the pre-dawn sky which was brightly lit up with stars. The stars here reminded me of the epitaph only a short distance from where we stood, 'Those are not stars in the sky but portals through which our little ones watch over us.'

The abandoned church whose roof was the stars with a floor of pebbles and neatly cut turf was now like a preserved monument. It held at least two hundred people in the pre-dawn of Easter Sunday. I couldn't help ignoring what the priest said because he seemed almost irrelevant in the setting. We were a community under the stars and had come to be with our ancestors, knowing our time would come only too soon. No representative of any world religion could say better in words what we already sensed as true inside us, standing waiting for night to pass and dawn to arrive. There was a sense of the limited number of sunrises we would see and I noticed most of the people there were in awe waiting for the sun to appear.

As I stood there in the slowly emerging dawn, two sounds brought my mind to a halt and I stood totally humbled. First the birds, out of nowhere, suddenly began tweeting, then whistling and then singing in a full chorus as if to rejoice the day and expectation of the sun. Everyone listened for about two minutes when they were interrupted suddenly by another sound. The birds stopped singing to listen to another sweet sound.

A teenage girl in an anorak, who was probably only thirteen years old, started playing a penny whistle perfectly. Suddenly there was silence. The birds stopped singing and stayed silent to listen to her for two minutes. She could be seen though everyone's visible breath in the icy cold air. Here was a simple communal consciousness uniting man with nature and the rising sun in memory of those who had already been absorbed back into the earth. This was true ancestor worship. When the young girl stopped playing the penny whistle, the birds erupted into even louder song than before.

Some religious words were said by the priest, then we all silently walked out on to the road and through the gates of Cloughan's to be at our family graves. The first rays of light from the early morning sun revealed the landscape I had forgotten. The graveyard faced the lock and on the other side of it was the granite mountain, now with its peak covered in snow. I remembered it from digging my uncle's grave with my daughter who had also come now to see the grave. Unlike the church which had been abandoned generations ago, the graves were not without human touch and care.

Religion had been repositioned in Ireland since I was a boy visiting there but this modern ritual showed that ancestor worship still guides many. I could already see that with the irreversible loss of its moral authority due to its scandal of secretly supporting corrupt criminal priests and nuns, the roofs would begin to fall in on other churches around the world.

I realised what I witnessed may have been a new local form of post Christian Neo Pagan ancestor worship.

A part of me wondered about this and I became concerned as I looked to the mountain in the distance because I imagined seeing a difficult future ahead. I was not sure if I was just looking at my own personal experience or if my experience was a warning of a future where we might once again have to do very basic things such as make the coffins and dig the graves for our loved ones.

28. Habits Which Become Addictive

Every day it seems we come across more and more people addicted to various activities or things. It could be that someone wants to control their appearance by weight loss, weight gain or by other cosmetic means. Perhaps because of modern technology the most recent addictions are more openly displayed. It could be someone's apparent need to always be on the phone, to constantly use a computer or to play computer games, to have more virtual friends or to gamble. Some addictions are so commonplace that they are acceptable to the point that in many cases it is now politically incorrect to even mention them.

Modern society has expanded the range of addictions so much that they could include a whole gamut of human behaviour. The most common ones are: anorexia, alcohol, bulimia, body building, cocaine, chocolate, crime, drugs not prescribed but available on the street such as glue, inhalants, solvents and legal highs, exercise, food, fetishes, gambling, heroin, internet, jogging, kleptomania, love, marijuana, nicotine, overeating, pornography, prescription drugs, quintessential behaviour (perfectionism), religion, social media, shopping, sex, self-harm, telephones, television, tattooing, underachieving, video games, wealth.

The naked truth behind addiction is dependence on the presumption that happiness comes solely from the exterior material world. Over-emphasis on the external conditions makes it much more difficult for people to access their inner selves. Thinking or rationalism has almost overwhelmed everything so that the inner aspect has been neglected. How has this come about?

Our superficial externalised cultures promote and encourage the acquisition of certain behaviours, experiences and possessions through all kinds of advertisements in the media using powerful role models. Many of these create desires which when fulfilled give the person the illusion of having obtained the accepted symbols of success. Some of these create the craving for more.

Similarly, people's appetite for technological progress in the external world is fuelled by their minds' desire for external knowledge so that they can control the external world and experience it to their liking and satisfaction. Their simple error is in doing this at the expense of their inner being. The desire of the mind to be dominant in everything overcomes their inner self which is eclipsed and withers. This results in a fatal loss of balance between the mind and the spirit.

The inner 'spiritual' world is the glue which when shared holds groups of men and women together and so when it is dissolved people become isolated and unhappy. This is when they let addictions move in . . . rent free.

Carl Jung was the first modern doctor to realise that medicine, psychology and psychotherapy do not work for people addicted to drugs or alcohol. Recently we have seen that this insight applies to many addictions.

On their last meeting in 1931, after many therapy sessions, Carl Jung informed his patient Rowland Hazzard of his 'hopelessness' as far as medical or psychiatric treatment was concerned in treating his addiction. Bluntly Jung wrote him off, making him conscious of his powerlessness over his addiction. However, Jung advised him that there might be hope for him if he became the subject of a religious or spiritual experience and if he placed himself in a religious atmosphere. Jung thus made Hazzard conscious of his powerlessness and of the option to surrender to a higher power.

This was an extraordinarily insightful and groundbreaking thing to do. Rowland Hazzard followed Jung's advice and completely recovered. Using Jung's advice Hazzard helped Bill Wilson to recover; Wilson in 1935 went on to co-found the first successful self-help group programme for recovering addicts, known today as AA or Alcoholics Anonymous. Bill Wilson said his conversation with Rowland Hazzard, his humility and deep perception played a critical role in the founding of the AA Fellowship.

In 1961, just months before Jung's death, Wilson wrote to thank Jung for his direct help in curing him of his addiction and his influence in helping to set up the first addiction recovery programme. Jung immediately replied informing him that he had taken a great risk at the time in advising Hazzard that the only hope left for him was to lead a spiritually based life in a community. For a medical doctor and psychiatrist to suggest a spiritual cure for addiction in 1931 was radically new and is probably why Jung did not mention it until after he was told about it by Wilson in 1961.

Most people believe that Jung's chief legacy was Analytical Psychology; a perspective which he hoped would take people further than religion in understanding themselves and making themselves whole. Many countries have several Jungian groups or Jungian societies. Jungian therapists influence thousands of people and Jung has been an enormously important contributor to modern psychology. However, his actual practical influence on humankind has been quite different to what he expected because it has primarily been in the field of addiction.

The Mechanism

Carl Jung in his reply to the 1961 letter from Bill Wilson said, "Alcohol in Latin is 'Spiritus', and you use the same word for the highest religious experience as well as for the most depraving poison. The helpful formula therefore is: Spiritus contra spiritum." Jung may have linked the two words together himself or he may have been displaying a condition he wrote about called 'cryptomnesia;' in which unknowingly he was quoting the Roman Caesar, Marcus Aurelius Antoninus (120-180 AD) who declared, 'Espiritum vinci espiritus.' Irrespective of this, both quotes mean the same, which is, spirit destroys spirit.

There are two ways of accessing the spirit; either the illusion of the spirit is invoked by alcohol, drugs, eating, gambling and sex, or the authentic spirit is invoked by the collapse of the ego and its surrender to the true self. This is the 'sense of the sacred.'

The lure of addiction gives people the feeling of

satisfaction and wholeness whilst in reality they are isolated and fragmented. They are experiencing not genuine wholeness of spirit but an imitation, a 'cuckoo' spirit. The cuckoo is a parasitic bird which in ten seconds can push an egg out of a nest and lay one of its own there to be hatched and nurtured by the host bird. When the cuckoo chick hatches it evicts the other chicks and is usually a giant compared to them causing massive problems to the host mother. In this biological 'arms race' the host mother adapts by changing the pattern on her eggs, specifically so that she can recognise them as her own, as opposed to the imitation egg placed there by a cuckoo. Similar to the host mother feeding the cuckoo chick, addicts are aware that they are harming themselves, but are compelled to continue to satisfy their craving. Likewise, their families and friends continue to support addicts even though they know that addiction harms them as well.

When people gather together, having decided to fight their addiction, a spirit is formed in the group which is a higher power than any individual can generate on his or her own. Just as the host mother uses nature to create an egg pattern which the cuckoo can't mimic, the spirit of solidarity formed and experienced in a community can shatter the illusion of satisfaction and wholeness that addictions create.

A supportive, nurturing community which encourages togetherness, understanding and spiritual meaning can inspire hope and encourage addicts to want to change their behaviours and belong more to the community. For many this may be the only path available to a sense of authentic wholeness. There is no actual cure, no medicine or therapy but there is hope.

This possibility of hope given to addicts by Jung in the form of spirituality in a group has probably had more influence on the world in the form of addiction groups than all the rest of Jung's work. It has probably contributed more to the healing of the sick than any form of psychological therapy. His contribution to mankind's spiritual development has not just been significant, it has been colossal and in a very different way to that which he imagined.

Therapy may be useful after recovery has started but therapy on its own doesn't produce a meaningful recovery from addictions as Jung and many since him have indicated. The most successful answers are in spiritually centred supportive communities such as Internet Anonymous, Television Anonymous, Narcotics Anonymous, Alcoholics Anonymous, Overeaters Anonymous for the addict and similar support groups for families and friends.

The Wider External World

The devastation is nowhere more obvious than in most of the native populations of North America and Australia whose spirit is still enshrined in their lands which they can no longer freely access. This is also becoming true in Tibet and in other lands where the natives' traditional connections with their sense of the spiritual through the earth are severed. Relocation, poverty, poor education, lack of prospects and opportunities could each be named as the culprit behind their addictions but this is not the original and ongoing cause. The true reason is that they have had their spiritual connection with the earth removed and they have had it replaced with a substitution of a false spirit composed of drugs or alcohol usually supplied by the thief who took their original true sense of wholeness and sacred integrity, a cuckoo spirit. The cuckoo spirit also inhabits and deeply affects family members and friends, disguising and taking over their true spirit.

It seems as if addiction has been weaponised to overcome whole nations which once flourished on and were proud of their spiritual life. For the people in these places the diet of the soul seems temporarily one-sided and overpowered by man's greed to obtain, own and control.

Families and Friends

Whatever the origin, addictions are a progressive disease of all the addicts' relationships. Addictions can't be controlled or cured, only arrested. Addiction is not just an individual illness because everyone in the family is deeply affected and unhappy. In some areas, whole communities and nations of people are deeply affected by addictions. Every family member leads a powerless life through the illusion that they cannot control the addict but the cuckoo spirit makes them keep on trying to change and control the addict.

In trying to stop the addict's drug taking/drinking or control their usage and in trying to make up for it, family members change emotionally, becoming disturbed themselves in reacting to the addict. They get stuck in a cycle of trying to have power over something which is unmanageable. They feel that they are being driven crazy.

There are always some similar patterns in all addicts and their families. Because there is no control over drugs, alcohol or other addictions, the addict's effects on everyone are chaotic and unpredictable with the result that everyone feels powerless. Unlike other diseases addiction is unmanageable and the people around the addict have to be over-vigilant and can't relax in normal ways and therefore can't relate in normal ways. They often become obsessional.

Family members and friends become different in the sense that they are not their 'full selves.' They remain emotionally confined and limited by the addicted person's behaviour. As well as fear and shame there is always resentment and anger. Unless family members are helped, this pattern of relating usually continues in their relationships with all others and extends for their whole life. Similarly, drug addiction/alcoholism not only devastates families, but also the next generation of children whose parents are handicapped because they themselves were brought up by an addicted parent.

Addicts may remain addicted as an emotional anaesthetic because they don't have the tools and the skills that are necessary to deal with emotions. Often they can't deal intelligently with their emotions because they weren't taught how to do so because they were brought up in an environment where a parent or grandparent was a drug taker or an alcoholic who was incompetent with his emotions.

Non-attachment

It is only when there is nowhere worse to be that their 'hopelessness' is recognised and help is sought by family's friends and the addicts. The well-meaning efforts of family members can stop addicts from getting the help they so desperately need. It is as if there has to be a 'gutter moment.' Likewise there may be a 'gutter moment' for family members and friends when they feel they will go crazy unless they leave the relationship or get some help. The naked truth about this time is best seen and understood by a parallel example in nature, as told in the following story, which I do not apologise for using a second time.

    A young boy found a cocoon and knowing what was inside it he brought it into his house where he waited for it to open up. He waited for hours looking at the cocoon. He eventually fell asleep and woke in the morning to find a hole had appeared in the cocoon. He watched it for a long time and finally in the afternoon a black leg appeared out of a hole struggling to make the hole bigger. There was little progress by the evening and so the boy thought he would help. He went to his Granny's sewing basket where he found a delicate pair of scissors that she used for crochet work. He went back to the cocoon where the leg was still struggling to open it. He delicately cut a line along the opening and out emerged the creature.

    He looked at it for a long time waiting for it to open its wings but it just seemed to wriggle about. Eventually he placed it by the open window where he thought the air would help it. He went off to ask his Granny for her help. She came back with him but the creature was lying on its back with its legs straight in the air as if dead. His Granny said, "When a butterfly is trying to get out of its cocoon, it struggles so hard that its heart beats faster and faster until its blood pressure gets very high. The very high pressure forces blood into the wings so that they open up, thus breaking open the cocoon. It is the only way a butterfly's wings can open."

The loved ones of drug addicts and alcoholics usually support their illnesses and cover up for all of their mistakes and shortcomings. But this only prolongs and prevents the addict and their family from getting proper help. Family and friends think they can control and cure the addictions but they are unmanageable diseases which can only be arrested.

Referring an addict for medical or psychological help usually wastes time because most doctors, psychiatrists and psychotherapists are not experts in this area. It is recovering addicts or recovering alcoholics themselves who are the experts. The proof is simply that they are 'clean' and sober and largely remain 'clean' and sober. Any other therapy is usually either a waste of time or will only eventually lead to Narcotics/Alcoholics Anonymous, so they might as well go straight to Narcotics/Alcoholics Anonymous to start with.

The drug addict/alcoholic may have some other problems which can be helped by therapy but this can only happen later on. The primary problem must be spelt out and acted on first; otherwise it risks, and may encourage, denial and avoidance and can perpetuate the problem. A person who goes to Narcotics Anonymous or Alcoholics Anonymous will learn something that they can learn no other way.

Most drug addicts or alcoholics who stop taking drugs or drink without using the resources offered for support and development by Narcotics/Alcoholics Anonymous remain as fragmented addicts or sober drunks. Usually their block in going to Narcotics/Alcoholics Anonymous is obsessional fear simply due to their lack of emotional tools and skills. Ironically Narcotics/Alcoholics Anonymous is just the place where they will find these emotional tools.

Similarly anyone who has had to suffer and endure living with a drug addict/alcoholic is usually wounded on so many levels of consciousness that there is no point in thinking they can get adequate help from well-meaning doctors, psychologists and psychotherapists. They are best helped by the friends and families of other drug addicts/alcoholics who have worked through this and who are therefore experts. They offer hope that there is a way out for families and friends to avoid being overwhelmed by a drug addict/alcoholic and their disease.

Families and friends need to understand how to deal with their emotions and their sense of their 'inner self'. They need to look again with another 'understanding family' to try to see the drug addiction/alcoholism with loving non-attachment. They can then reconnect with others, their 'inner self' and their sense of the sacred. Their boundaries, attitudes and relationships can then at last begin to improve as they recover.

Recovery

Recovery is really based on four principal ideas. The first is that as an addict or a family member you are utterly 'powerless' over drugs, alcohol or any other addiction. The second is that because of this the only choice is to turn to something bigger than yourself...your own sense of spirituality, the sacred or a higher power. For some this higher power may be just the power of the group they go to. The third is realising that your thinking, in its attitudes and behaviours has been disturbed by the addiction or the addict and you accept that you want to change your attitudes and behaviour. The fourth is that you can only keep the gift of healing that you have received if you give it away by helping others.

Perhaps the most liberating principle of 12 step programmes for addictions is religious freedom . . . freedom from religion. It can be anything you see it as. This unifying principle has been echoed repeatedly. On the portals of the temple of Delphi were written two things. "Everything in moderation and Know the self." Christ said, "The kingdom of God is within." Shakespeare said, "This above all-to thine own self be true, and it must follow as the night the day thou canst not be false to any man." Vivekananda said, "It is a blessing to be born in to a religion and a tragedy to die in one." Ramana Maharshi said "Happiness is your nature. It is not wrong to desire it. What is wrong is seeking it outside when it is inside." I would add, "Religion encourages doing a deal with God about the future - spirituality encourages living the deal now."

29. Virtual Reality and Technology

In 1984 I was asked by Phil Judkins from the Xerox Corporation, to look at the possible psychological effects of using new computer technology. The computer was The Star Workstation, officially known as the Xerox 8010 Information System. The Star was introduced by Xerox Corporation in 1981 and was the first computer to incorporate various technologies that have since become standard in personal computers, including a bitmapped display, a window based graphical user interface, icons, folders, mouse (two-button) Ethernet networking, file servers, print servers and e-mail. The Star represented a milestone in the human computer interface which was thought of as a step towards developing virtual reality computer systems.

After discussions with leading IT people of the day, doctors and psychologists, a research study was designed and undertaken by myself and John Heron, (the pioneering clinical psychologist) on a group of 21 people who were using The Star for 8 hours a day. The subjects were also assessed by us and also by a counsellor and a physiotherapist for all known effects of stress including physiological measurement such as blood pressure and detailed blood analysis.

At the end of the research, the unanimous conclusion was that using this technology for 8 hours a day did not lead to any form of stress which could be detected. I decided not to publish the research findings.

If the same research was conducted today on a similar group of people, the findings would probably be the same. The main reason for this seems to be that it is not the use of computers at work which seem to have changed us but more the double use injury or multiple use injury. Musicians hardly ever injure themselves simply from playing their instruments because they have trained to have the stamina to do so. However, musicians who also use their hands with considerable effort in their spare time such as painting ceilings or doing manual work frequently sustain a 'double use injury' which is not immediately apparent except through careful questioning.

Similarly, the average person using a computer during the working day seems to come to no psychological harm but using other forms of similar technology such as smart phones or tablets in the evenings may lead to simple multiple use fatigue. But this is not all there is to the effects of modern technology because in using them we are immersing ourselves in virtual worlds.

Overuse or over-immersion in virtual worlds outside of 'working hours' may be encouraged as a normal way of occupying our time especially by those who benefit from us doing so. Over-immersion can be an easy escape from the real world of having to interact with family and friends. For some can be an easier way to feel more comfortable experiencing less pain and discomfort than in the real world. Over-immersion in a virtual world may become our easiest 'default' way of occupying time so that eventually we become self programmed to plug into this virtual world, over-immersing in it to the point where the virtual world acts like a drug, numbing us like any opiate and therefore avoiding experiencing real feelings.

Our experience of the real world can be so reduced that our interaction with nature and with real people in real time and space may be so little as to be almost absent.

The absence of relating to nature and to real people in real time and space removes the benefits these things give us. We are then in a situation where we are not relating to people and not getting the nurturing that this brings, but also without the contrasting problems relating always brings.

It is over thirty years since the Xerox research project on the Star and we have in that time become proficient at multi-tasking with two or three of these devices at the same time. Today a person may use a laptop, tablet, smart-phone, smart watch, eyeglasses, contact lenses or heads up display (HUDS) to communicate with hundreds to millions of people by e-mail, Facebook, Facetime, Twitter, Instagram, Snapchat or other electronic formats. They may use these through all waking hours, at work, in education, at home, in intimate relationships, for business, for sex, for religion, for entertainment, as leisure, as therapy or in criminal ways.

With these devices a funeral can be relayed to absent relatives who may not be able to travel, wherever they may be in the world. And although this may be seen as progress, it comes with the loss of many things and can leave only a second rate reality to life. A person attending an e-funeral has not travelled and thought about the journey to the deceased and loved ones. They cannot meet, greet and hold the people in mourning and give them the warmth of their hands or their embrace. They cannot share the experience of being there as much as they cannot smell the flowers or be with the deceased on their last journey. They cannot throw that flower onto the coffin.

The loss of basic experiences is a serious challenge and a threat to mankind, because, by permitting the entry of technology into our lives to help us we may have removed experiences; and this reduces not only our understanding but also our feelings about people, places and things. It may be making us behave less autonomously and more like automated machines.

Technology has enabled us to communicate instantly with almost anyone anywhere and at a tiny cost and there have been great advances in access to information, in medicine and travel. But is this progress in that our quality of life is better? Are we as prosperous as we have been in that we are flourishing, thriving, happy, healthy and in a state of good fortune?

The extraordinary technology which children have easy access to in order to gather and process information has also unfortunately been used by the media to over-promote competitiveness rather than cooperativeness, greed rather than sharing, power rather than empowering and worship of celebrity status rather than equality. In the past values such as honesty, compassion and humility were promoted and nurtured by parents at home, teachers at school and religious figures in temples. Over the years these parents, teachers and inner guides have been pushed to the side by other things such as psychology, the new age and finally new technologies. So we have the responsibility of being in a crisis about our core values which should define us as co-operative civilised humans. Technology plays a significant role in this.

Perhaps we are becoming more 'down and out.' Maybe we have been moving downwards as opposed to upwards in that we are not flourishing, as we are not thriving, we are less happy, we are unhealthy and in a worse state of good fortune. Man's sight and perception are more focused on going more outwards (more superficial and materialistic) as opposed to inwards (more spiritual).

As already mentioned, in their advanced training, members of the armed forces, such as air crew and special forces, who are at the highest risk of falling into enemy hands, have to re-learn basic survival skills, such as how to find water, food and shelter, and learn to live whilst hiding and evading capture. To primitive man the use of these skills were automatic, everyday experiences. In the world's most advanced countries (UK, USA, Canada, Australia and New Zealand) air crew, Special Forces and secret service agents now have to spend weeks learning these essential skills on specialist Survival, Escape, Resistance and Escape (SERE) courses. That it is only the most advanced countries that have to do this is indicative of the fact that technological advance is often accompanied by a loss of fundamental self-reliance.

It is common to overindulge in the use of technology to the point of binge use. We are already at a point where technology substitutes everyday experiences. Even corporate mindfulness courses are on line. Already some individuals are having to go on specialised courses to learn how to be in a room with family or friends for prolonged periods without resorting to technology. Some have to go on courses to learn how to be able to have a meaningful intimate relationship. Others have to go on courses to learn how to spend leisure time without technology so that they can relax and psychologically decompress.

If we have to go back to classes to re-learn how to be friends, how to relate to people, how to be gentle and kind and how to enjoy life, then what have we become? We just haven't realised the position we are in because the consequences have not been seen or felt on a large enough scale nor made a significant impact to make us want to do something about it.

Technology, in the form of simple tools, originally helped man to survive. A rock could help fight off an assailant, whether another man or a beast. A rock could also be used in the form of an arrowhead to kill an animal for food. A metal rock changed by heat could be used to cut wood for a timber shelter. Technology might one day be able to transport us to distant planets to set up new civilisations. It may even let us preserve the ways our brains think in a memory device. But it won't be able to preserve our 'sense of the spiritual, our consciousness, our inner self.'

For some of us, because it seems easier to relate to artificial intelligence than to people, we choose to relate to artificial intelligence rather than to people. We might ask, 'What is new about mankind being this dependent on technology?' The answer is that if we program ourselves to do this for long enough, eventually we might lose our very nature, ceasing to know and be what we know as human and become artificially intelligent. Perhaps we are only just beginning to see that we are programming our minds to do this and we are taking steps to use technology less and to be less dependent on it.

Notes From The Inside

30. Living in the Present

This is the exact time of your life. The moment now is the only present time you will ever experience. Do you live in the present moment, conscious of the life of your limited time here, conscious of existing today? It is so much easier to live in the future. It is worth considering that we can choose to live in the future as an escape, an escape from living in the present right now. Coming at us today is the unknown, things about the future which could leave us in a mess if we ignore the present. Today is the only day we will ever have as the rest are an illusion to keep us from the present.

Why shouldn't today be the happiest you have ever been, because happiness comes from inside. Yes, you create it by being conscious of it. It is only up to you if you want to be your happiest ever. Somewhere happiness is inside us and it is always the same, with the same potential to change us. It is just we can't see this.

The present is a critical time. Critical times are always now. A critical time calls for completely focused watching and listening before action. Everything else is ditched to survive. All of life can seem critical, not a moment to waste on what is not necessary to survive fully conscious. Imagine today is your last day of life. All you need is what you need for today because you can only be as happy as you can be today. This is how we can see every day.

All our yesterdays and tomorrows are taken care of if we live in the present. To stay in the present, we need to find out how to let the past and future just be. Seeing what was and what I went through all those years ago, I can go through it again and again in my mind today because time is a great illusion of the mind.

The present is being attentive now but only you can be present. No one can give it to you as you have to be fully here not distracted. The future is not ours to focus on and to worry about. It is a waste of energy worrying about the future. If we focus more about what we are doing now, the future will always be sorted out. It is not ours.

We hold some time in the future. Maybe it is an event, an age or even our death but we have something we know of here which is also of there which we know is inevitable. It is our self.

There are layers to the sky and layers to the stars and there are layers of our consciousness. Standing under the night sky we see this more clearly. The apparent sense of being conscious of time passing is not the sense of passing time but consciousness of being.

You can offer all the things all the experiences to explain everything. At the end you have to come back to your inner self. The world has not changed as the plants and animals come and go struggling with each other simply to bathe in the light.

The weather inside over the next few hours is as far as I go into the future. Tomorrow and next week will be taken care of for us all, inside and out. We may not need to remove hope but we cannot lie; the truth is usually simple hope complicated.

31. Creativity

At some time we decide to do something to stop thinking, to slow and stop the tide of rationalism. We decide to show that thinking is not the only way to express the most important aspects of our self and our inner self.

Early experiences of distressing thoughts and feelings, the pain of abuse, the pain of loss or of abandonment are sometimes best expressed through drawing, painting, sculpting, singing, music or writing. They help us express and understand our memories, our thoughts and feelings and can also help to communicate our love, friendship, kindness and our inner self. Creativity is probably the most healing of all things to be immersed in.

We can write, draw, sing and paint with a child-like naivety which indirectly shows us and others trying to help us, what we cannot express directly, perhaps because it is too difficult or painful to express directly.

Inspiration does not come from nowhere. Usually you think you might be able to do something better or just dare yourself to solve a problem or show it in a different way. You have already started the work. Then, falling asleep or engaged in something ordinary, you find yourself on a pathway which has just opened up in front of you. You are conscious you are on your own and feel alone with a hundred thousand pairs of eyes looking down on you, wanting to look up at you.

Taking risks, the mistakes are not mines trying to destroy you but only there to annoy you and encourage progress. Leaving forgiveness behind, exploring what is not allowed, encourages further exploration. Perfection is the enemy of progress because it stifles looking further. Perfection halts all growth whereas progress with imperfection is the growth process. Failure is one of the best motivators and the best place to start from time and time again as failure is always available. Failure is begging for change, begging for improvement. Failure has the greatest potential, more potential than success.

We seem like such creatures of habit but only in some

things sometimes. We go for the same breakfasts, stay with the same people. Our minds are conditioned from the past to make the future secure, predictable, paradisiacal, and comfortable with no inconvenience, discomfort or pain. Only artists are forced to experiment with themselves and their art. Some are already but some become what their art will show. Comfort is stifling, so fear of discomfort is turned into fuel to go even further to see what happens, where they can go. Some can sing the love. Some can paint the pain. Some can sculpt a hole so deep it seems like you'll never get out again. But there are those who imagine what we can only dream and they directly show our eyes what our hearts have not yet seen.

Our view of the world is like the artist and the canvas; the canvas should not paint the artist. Meeting artists is like meeting musicians as they are usually not like anything which they present and why should they be because they have taken a tortuous route to contort, not resorted to what we take for granted. The straight line of all the lines is the worst. It has to be straight not bent. It ruins the line of things which could be curved and better for the eye to observe. The body has got no straight lines. Nature is not sophisticated to be so poorly defined.

I used to believe in songs. I used to love anthems of our lives, of our times. But these come and go and like the people driven to write the lines, they are part of our growing up and moving on. To have what the singer says you can find, you can't as they say, 'keep on becoming.' You have to stop and be still. Maybe we should stop trying to become and instead just be still.

The best words worth reading, the best poems worth writing, the best songs worth hearing are natural, those of spirit. Hearing all the songs, all the music, all the poetry, all the stories in all the books point the way to being our inner self, which is there all along. All the best songs, poems and art are not about us; they are us. Songs sing only of our love for others in our self. Poems speak of our love of the world in our self. Art displays to others the love we could have for our self. The poet seems like no hero but instead like a soldier trying to show us things no one else can see. It is not the paint or the brush that outlines the love; it's the stroke of the hand which weaves the story from the heart. It is the presence of the heart we see in the stroke of the hand that draws and on the lips that sing.

It is impossible to express the relief of not having to write for anyone else, only just writing for you. We usually don't realise until late on that we need to write just for us. Saying how happy we are in words doesn't reflect clearly enough how we see things. Beauty is something recognised outside, happiness is always inside. Beauty is delivered from the senses, happiness is revealed inside. Beauty is a synthesis of fine thinking; happiness is simply being in the heart.

Artists get taken over, their free time, their holiday spent compelled to sing, draw or write in silence whatever comes into the heart or into the mind. That which seems important has to be written, sung or drawn. No sleep-in to be lazy because it is life's work being shown.

It's not even breakfast yet and a lot of an artist's day's work is done. All the thinking is done. The day to enjoy is now here. Artists know the early morning light is best because few people get out of bed to see it. It looks more unusual simply because the light comes from the other side. The morning is best to see most things. The night brings shadows of fear, illusions which are only clear again in the morning light. This is why any decisions about work or letters should always be slept on, so there is a fresh different morning light on them. We should also step back as we become so fixated on what we decide to do, we can forget to enjoy the moments from the decision until we actually achieve it. We should try and have the pleasure of the work before the time for pleasure of the work has gone.

Notes From The Inside

32. What Makes Us Choose

Wherever I was, I have wanted to have and give a sense of the inner self, the spirit within. So this is the path I took and am still on. At first this was not so simple because thinking, especially clever thinking, complicated things for me by trying to throw me off the scent of my path. It looked like there were different paths I should be taking. I was confused because there seemed to be two different paths.

The path going one way is the path of the intellect. The path going the other way is the path of surrender. I turned one way, thought so much and couldn't work it out, so I gave up and took the path going the other way; the path of surrender. Having surrendered, I now completely understand the path going one way eventually joins with the path going the other way. Whichever one you choose takes you to the same place.

Even though I ended up on the opposite path, which was my second choice, my second choice was the best. My first choice was the best, then my second choice was. They seemed different but now they are the same. They can only ever merge into one path. The point of breakthrough was seeing that the path I took was the right one all the time. We can only see the road we are on not the one ahead. The path we are on is the only one that can lead to the one ahead. Whichever way you go, all paths lead you to the same final path. Whichever way you go, it will be on your own path, nobody else's path.

One of the other most helpful things was to see that the path we are on is actually the goal. The goal we seek is none other than the path we are on.

We are biologically, psychologically and emotionally the same but spiritually we take different paths. Perhaps it is not us but the planet's different characteristics which forge our feeling of what is spiritually significant. Is it the mountains, the rivers, how the sun rises and sets over the lands or is it some combination of things which turn us inwards to see the inner self? Our understanding of the connections between all these and us is like a child's understanding.

However odd I may seem, however wrong in my choices, it is right just to be me. There is a strange intuition behind my choices which I cannot explain, only the outcome can. We can sit around doing nothing or we can sit around trying to be happy by the only means we know. It is your choice to leave behind your happiness, your nature and your smile.

Your thoughts are original. They are your own unique thoughts. But they are just thoughts. They are only thoughts. They are common quite usual thoughts which we have been having for tens of thousands of years. You think that your thoughts make you behave like you want to but are you sure? Maybe you are going through the thinking motions which ensure what is supposed to happen will happen. When we seem to choose, perhaps it was already so. It is a belief that we choose and it is also a belief that we don't choose. It is a belief that choice indicates no predestination. But choice may not in truth be optional. Truth is not a choice.

As knowing what it is to be a parent can only be known by being a parent, so truth can only be known by being true to your inner self. You only need to be true to you. There is no one else you need to be true to. Not to the written word, neither to stories, books, nor to the world of comings and goings; only to you. Not to the teacher, preacher or doctor; neither to subjects, only you.

We are distracted by being attracted to complexity not simplicity, to noise not silence, to movement not stillness, to resistance rather than acceptance, to desire not happiness. We are attracted to thinking rather than being still, to importance not humility, to personality not principles, to gaining rather than sharing, to looking out not in. We are attracted to the future not the present, to speech not the grace of silence, to style not content, to competitiveness not cooperation, to separateness not compassion. We are attracted to distractions rather than non-attachment, to seeing parts not everything, to the many not the few, to the popular not the outsiders, to dividing rather than bringing together. We are attracted to mystery not truth, to doing not being, to emotions not love, to power not friendliness, to distractions rather than non-attachment.

In summary, we are attracted to complexity not simplicity, to thinking rather than being still, to the future not the present, to attachment rather than non-attachment, to mystery not truth. The essence is 'Simply be still now non-attached true to your inner self.' It is our choice.

Because the majority supports a person doesn't mean they are right. A whole country can support something and be wrong about it but be right about supporting each other. Best not to get involved. Get on with your own life leaving others' lives and concerns alone, seeing only the positive merits, overlooking other's faults. What you do for someone you really do for you so do it perfectly.

Brothers and sisters like to compete to find out and show you who they are and by joining in you find more about you as well. But as adults not leaving things like this behind when there should be more serious things on their minds is childish. If the relationship is subtle combat and continues without development, eventually there is no choice but to leave and be with friends.

Maybe everything is just as it should be and we should stop thinking how to change it. Non-acceptance can be our greatest enemy, acceptance our waiting friend. If we accepted life we would have less to do, more time for peace and more to just be still. Do you want to leave something behind, a trace? All traces will eventually go so do you want to spend time leaving a trace. Our pattern is not seen until we have nearly completed it, our impact usually not until we have gone.

If we drop our expectations of someone, accepting them for what they are and not trying to change them, we have less of a problem. Dropping expectations doesn't lesson us but lets us grow wiser branches for others to settle on. Our nurturing is our choice.

When you are young in your teens you choose your nurturing, what you feed off and live on. You can either live a life of chaotic messy descent or of a disciplined inner life of being consciously happy in your stillness. At first decay is only slight but all the slight choices of decay add up and as you start to feel unwell, others begin to notice. You isolate yourself with your choices until everyone has gone. If you choose the inner disciplined life, at first growth is only slight but all the choices add up and as you start to feel happy, others begin to notice. You become part of others and everything.

Why do we sometimes appear to choose unwisely? Why do some of us become addicted to drugs or alcohol? Are we copying someone, a parent, a hero or a friend? It is easy not to be happy, so easy to be sad. What persuades us is not worth more than us. Maybe we choose suffering because we need to learn from it that we are actually miserable and unhappy and it is going to show us what real happiness is.

Information you are given as a warning or guidance doesn't usually help, perhaps because it is your destiny that drives you, not your head. Whatever you do leads you there. Whatever you don't do leads you there, just the same.

We think we have control over our world because we want to have control over our world. But we can also see our world has its own form, movement and intentions because it is not ours. When you are uninjured but others are not, when you survive and others do not, you cannot look at these incidents without seeing fate having a hand as none of you chose to live or die.

Past and future are words we use to describe thoughts of what is. Past and future are only words we can use to understand fate. Perhaps past and future are only other words for fate.

Eventually you see you have been following a scent. You have been listening for truth. You have been watching for it, waiting for it. It is the stillness here inside you. Then you see your journey has taken care of you, the path leading to a holy place, a sacred mountain, they are your stillness.

What is worth making a decision about when it was all decided long ago? Fate is not anything like a power in control. It is not something that can be named. Everything can be fate. Fate is what things are meant to be as they are.

When we are overwhelmed by great change which we have no control over, how do we change and adapt in the face of apparent powerlessness? The American Indian Chief Plenty Coups (1848-1932) had a strong reputation as a war chief and was a feared warrior but he knew he had to give all of this up and radically change in the face of the 'white man's' inevitable settlement of his reservation. Basically, he had to accept defeat as he couldn't change the settlement of the 'white man' and he had to surrender to this. But he saw that he could make changes which enabled him to adjust to living with them.

When threatened with the inevitable settlement of the 'white man' on the reservations, Plenty Coups had a dream in which he saw the buffalo disappear and be replaced with spotted cattle (the 'white man') and the forest destroyed by a storm except for just one single tree which was occupied by a tribe who had built their lodge beside it. This tribe were known for their listening and co-operation. This dream was said to have guided Plenty Coups to lead his tribe from the 'buffalo days' through the days of 'reservation settlement.' During this time, he settled down, started farming, opened a store and built a two-story house.

So, what about us, when we are overwhelmed by great loss or change which we have no control over? First we need to see what we are powerless over, because it is usually not everything. We have to see we are defeated and surrender to this and then accept it. But we also have to see there are some things we can do to help us adjust to what we have no control over. Acceptance of our powerlessness and surrendering goes a long way to help our calmness and composure, whilst the inevitable happens. Acceptance of defeat and surrendering opens the way to inner peace.

When we are threatened with being overwhelmed by the inevitable collapse of what we thought we knew was stable, there is no single reaction because we react in a variety of ways. Whichever way we react we are trying to cope and restore balance to our life so we can maintain a state of happiness. Our reactions are temporary to get us to the stage which is acceptance. We may get angry. We can get stuck in denial as a way of buffering things which are too uncomfortable to accept yet. We can become anxious, depressed or appear to be in other altered states of consciousness, but eventually we find acceptance and peace.

My friend Narikutti had a guru, 'Yogaswami of Jaffna,' who used to say only four things: '1. All is truth. 2. There is not even one wrong thing. 3. We do not know. 4. It was all accomplished long ago.'

We are more powerless than we want to admit, so surrendering helps us to be calm and composed producing an inner serenity of surrender. This is most important in a crisis, if we want to survive.

Our life can seem like a long drawn out play with the characters people we know, playing their parts with us. Surprising us with their scripts and moves which seem written long before because perhaps we already know the ending.

Just like soldiers in denial, in order to buffer and avoid acceptance, we think it won't be us but wave after wave of us fall. There are never any exceptions to how fate is not just first and last but everything before in between and after. Returning to stillness is our origin and fate.

No worries about securities make life easy for everyone with no talking of money or its consequences. People, family and friends, if you have any, do you believe they are not looked after or are their fate and ours already sealed? Do you think you can control their fate? Is this possible, that you can leave it all up to fate or some other power and be foolish, free and happy to just be? Can you let go of everything and just let go of trying to control all outcomes? Maybe it is your biggest choice.

33. From the Mind to the Inner Self

You don't need a clever doctor. You don't need a psychologist or psychiatrist. You don't need anyone to tell you that you need to control your own mind. It is the simplest thing of all to miss that can leave us all in a mess, not seeing we are responsible for being in control of our mind. How can these thoughts stop bothering me so I can be in control? How can these thoughts be stopped? Mind control is the most important answer to look for. It can cure all kinds of distress. Mind control is about controlling only our mind, not other's minds. The aim is to not let thoughts control us and to be peaceful without them. We have to find out how to be still inside without thoughts.

Just when I can't think of anything else and I feel that's the day done, something crops up and it finds its life on a page. How strange that we let thoughts keep on forming which then search for words to become sentences which can be written or spoken. What we don't seem to see is that stopping thoughts is a more important job.

One thing can stop us thinking. Our thinking can be overwhelmed by a daily dose of our favourite drug, taken each night at the same time; our sleep. It is only by seeing there is self and non self and everything is either self or not self that everything is seen as self. There are no unwanted side effects. No one else is involved. You make a full recovery until you need more. It is sedation and lets you sleep. It gives you an altered state of consciousness.

In the West what we don't know about us we call the unconscious, in the East we call it the self. Neither is right nor wrong, only names for our ignorance. This is how I see it. Ignorance is what we don't know about our inner self. What we don't know is that we already have all the happiness inside us today. Ignorance is not having seen this. When we see it, our ignorance is removed.

With ignorance we are searching for happiness. Without ignorance the search is called off. With ignorance our thoughts are in control. Without ignorance we are happy without thoughts.

With ignorance we suffer in the outside world. Without ignorance we are happy inside. With ignorance we try to control outcomes. Without ignorance surrender is complete. With ignorance we are busy in the world. Without ignorance we have detached.

Some people seem to wake and change in their teens, others in their twenties, thirties or in a late decade but when darkness is removed and they wake up, ignorance has started to go. For some there is only one purpose left, the desire to see completely, to have ignorance fully removed.

You may have a certain attitude to want to be in a special place for detachment, solitude and silence. But to enquire, surrender, to remove ignorance and to be still in happiness, no special place is needed.

There comes a time invited or not when you leave everything behind. It is merging with your inner self, detachment from all else. But unseen it is a merging with everything else. Because of the connections not seen it is the final removal of darkness so connectedness is seen everywhere.

The more you know the more you know you don't know. The more effort the less effort is required until there is none. The more you see the more you see there is nothing to see. The more you hear the more you hear nothing to hear.

We have all probably been in the presence of some good people, perhaps some of them were great people. We have come across the traces left by others who perhaps were great people. Simplicity is often a sign there may be greatness. Humility is another sign but compassion is the energy of the great whilst getting on with their work. I like people for their hearts, not for their thoughts. You can call it the inner self anything you like but that is what I like. Minds are like machines varied, sometimes impressive but they cannot just be the inner self.

I am so happy I never valued thinking much and never gave it control as my mind would have taken over the direction of my heart. So how do I forget to remind myself to be happy so often, because I forget to be happy all the time? There is no reason other than reason getting in the way.

There are moments sometimes lasting seconds or

minutes, rarely all morning or afternoon when everything in life is perfect, not a single thing is wrong. These moments can sometimes be created by not thinking, so we have to remind our self to choose them.

On Saturday afternoons there is usually a sense of enjoyment before Sunday's solemnity, the fun before the regrouping of serious thoughts ready for the week of work. In some places there are no weekends, no particular days to the week, no holidays, holy days on or off days, just days of great peace.

The most interesting aspect of other people's lives is often how they found out about themselves, how they discovered consciousness; the permanent aspect of their life. It is the inner weather whose inner directed wind has only one aim, only a single purpose; happiness. Having turned away forever from where happiness cannot be found, because it is a clever illusion, there is nowhere else to go except inside. Stormy outer weather continues, whilst inside there is always calmness in the refuge.

34. Being Still

Problems in the world and fear of outcomes become meaningless in being still. The crushing weight of missed personal opportunities may have added up in our past but become meaningless in being still. Isolation and the lack of previous joyful activities all become meaningless in being still.

The suffering of lost friends, missed ancestors, the pain of disease, and loss of tears of happiness become meaningless in being still. What we are with complete surrender is being still. Enquiry into our self with complete surrender, practicing kindness let stillness be seen as truth.

With being alive there is often prolonged physical ill health, being attacked by our thoughts, disturbances from within by frustration and disillusionment, loss of faith, hopelessness, helplessness, and the pain of loss. But always alongside these is our sense of something permanent; our sense of that which always is. Our ability to experience this stillness as consciousness, as the inner self, eclipses everything we can think. It is simply being still.

Nothing is better than being happy in the stillness of our inner self which remains. Celebrity status, recognition of intellectual eloquence, influence or securities are worldly expressions of superficial happiness which all pass.

The stillness of solitude is the gift everyone wants but it can't be given. Stillness is the most priceless jewel which few can easily access. The stillness of solitude is free in exchange for the effort of looking inside. The inner treasury room is priceless.

A torturer cannot take away from us what can only be seen by us. How do we cope when we are turned upside down, when we lose our bearings, rudderless, unable to anchor ourselves to anything secure? Where our anchor lies most secure is being still, not subject to winds of change; central and still, not moved by anyone; in our inner harbour.

Eventually you see you have been following a scent. You have been listening for truth. You have been watching for it, waiting for it. Then you see your journey has taken care of you.

There is no sacred mountain. There is no path. They are all just stillness, just as you are here now.

Eventually you see that looking for a wise person who can guide you comes from your desire to find your own inner wise guide; to find him or her in your inner self. If you can bring her or him up inside as your inner self, this is the greatest gift you can ever have as the presence of the inner guide is your very nature.

Returning to seeing that you have been caught up in thinking and that you have not been still is the return to consciousness from reduced consciousness. Our inability to concentrate on being still is our greatest weakness; being still our greatest treasure.

It may be that there comes a time when we discover a difficult aspect of the way we are living. We see we are restlessly addicted to change or to changing thoughts, which can only be resolved by being still.

Somehow between our thoughts, stillness is discovered which we recognise as our inner happiness. Whatever way we reach this stillness and surrender to it, is our own meditation, and is the removal of our ignorance leading to happiness.

The gap between thoughts when found, through whatever mind control method of distracting and stopping thoughts, is the aim of all. The stillness in the gap between thoughts is what we seek, the ultimate of all forms of our happiness. It is the essence of us. The stillness in the gap between thoughts is our truth, is the truth common to all. It is our own spirit.